ATLAS OF
AMERICAN HISTORY

BOOKS BY MARTIN GILBERT

The Churchill Biography

Volume III, 'The Challenge of War', 1914–1916
Volume III, Documents, Parts I and II
Volume IV, 'The Stricken World', 1916–1922
Volume IV, Documents, Parts I, II and III
Volume V, 'The Prophet of Truth', 1922–1939
The Exchequer Years, Documents, 1924–1929
The Wilderness Years, Documents, 1929–1935
The Coming of War, Documents, 1936–1939
Volume VI, 'Finest Hour', 1939–1941
Volume VII, 'Road to Victory', 1941–1945
Volume VIII, 'World in Torment', 1945–1965 (*in preparation*)

Historical works

The Appeasers (with Richard Gott)
The European Powers 1900–1945
Churchill: A Photographic Portrait
Sir Horace Rumbold: Portrait of a Diplomat
Exile and Return: the Emergence of Jewish Statehood
Final Journey: The Fate of the Jews of Nazi Europe
Auschwitz and the Allies: the Politics of Rescue
The Jews of Hope: The Plight of Soviet Jewry Today
Jerusalem: Rebirth of a City, 1838–1898
Holocaust: A History of the Jews of Europe during the Second World War

Editions of documents

Britain and Germany Between the Wars
Plough My Own Furrow, The Life of Lord Allen of Hurtwood
Servant of India: Diaries of the Viceroy's Private Secretary
Churchill (Spectrum Books: Great Lives Observed)
Lloyd George (Spectrum Books: Great Lives Observed)

Atlases

Recent History Atlas, 1860–1960
British History Atlas
American History Atlas
Jewish History Atlas
First World War Atlas
The Arab-Israeli Conflict: Its History in Maps
The Jews of Arab Lands: Their History in Maps
The Jews of Russia: Their History in Maps
Jerusalem: Illustrated History Atlas
Imperial Russian History Atlas
Soviet History Atlas
Children's Illustrated Bible Atlas
Atlas of the Holocaust

ATLAS OF
AMERICAN HISTORY

REVISED EDITION

MARTIN GILBERT

Fellow of Merton College, Oxford

Cartography by ARTHUR BANKS and TERRY BICKNELL

DORSET PRESS

Library of Congress Catalog Card Number: 71-85777

1985 Dorset Press

This edition published by Dorset Press, a division of MARBORO BOOKS Corp. by arrangement with the proprietor. Originally published as *American History Atlas.*

American History Atlas was first published in Great Britain in 1968 by Weidenfeld and Nicolson, London

ISBN 0-88029-058-7
(Previously ISBN 0-88029-016-1)

Printed in the United States of America

2 3 4 5 6 7 8 9 10

Preface

The idea for this atlas came to me while I was teaching at the University of South Carolina. Its aim is to provide a short but informative visual guide to American history. I have tried to make use of maps in the widest possible way, designing each one individually, and seeking to transform statistics and facts into something easily seen and grasped. My material has been obtained from a wide range of historical works, encyclopaedias and newspaper reports. I have tried to be as comprehensive as possible, consistent with clarity; only the reader can judge if I have succeeded.

More than fifteen years have passed since the first publication of this atlas. It was a period marked first by the intensification and then by the ending of the Vietnam war, with more than 55,000 American dead. It was also a period marked by a substantial increase in the population of the United States, and continued immigration. This same period has seen the development of outer space as a region of defence policy. New maps cover these recent developments.

I am grateful in this new edition to the cartographic skills of Mr Terry Bicknell, and I should once more welcome any notice of errors and suggestions for further maps.

MARTIN GILBERT
5 February 1985, Merton College, Oxford

List of Maps

ATLAS OF
AMERICAN HISTORY

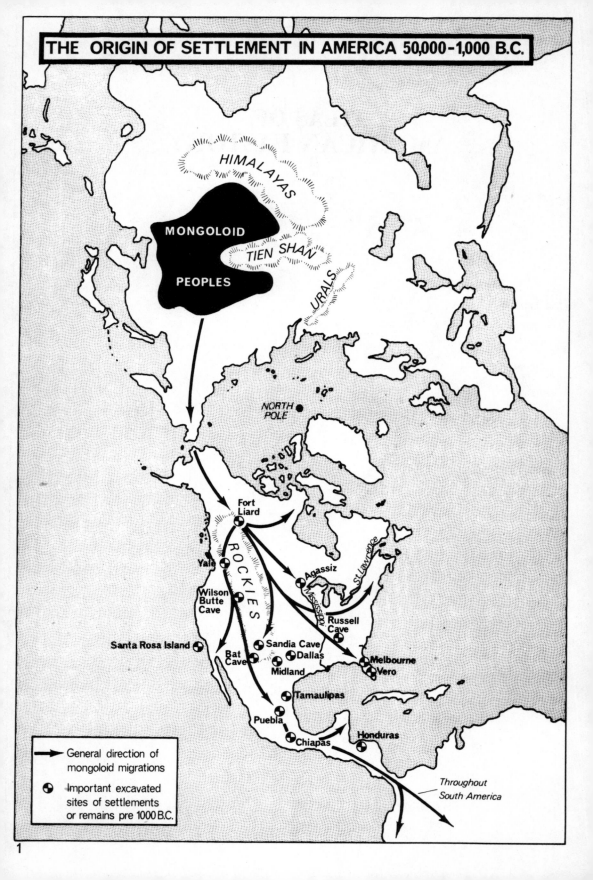

THE ORIGIN OF SETTLEMENT IN AMERICA 50,000-1,000 B.C.

HIMALAYAS

MONGOLOID

TIEN SHAN

PEOPLES

URALS

NORTH POLE

Fort Liard

Yale

ROCKIES

Wilson Butte Cave

Agassiz

St. Lawrence

Mississippi

Russell Cave

Santa Rosa Island

Sandia Cave

Dallas

Bat Cave

Midland

Melbourne

Vero

Tamaulipas

Puebla

Chiapas

Honduras

General direction of mongoloid migrations

Important excavated sites of settlements or remains pre 1000 B.C.

Throughout South America

1

THE INDIAN TRIBES OF NORTH AMERICA BEFORE 1492

Eskimo
Koyukon
Ingalik
Tanaina
Aleut

Kutchin
Han
Tanana
Nabesna
Tuchone
Ahtena
Kaska
Tahltan
Tlingit

Hare
Bear Lake
Dogrib
Yellowknife
Slave
Sekani
Beaver

Eskimo

Chipewyan

Tsimshian
Bella Coola
Haida
Bella Bella
Kwakiutl
Nootka
Salish
Makah Puyallup
Nisqually
Chehalis
Chinook
Cowlitz
Tillamook
Yakima
Klikitat
Molala
Kalapuya
Coos
Umpqua
Takelma
Karok
Yurok
Wiyot
Shasta
Hupa
Yana
Mattole
Maidu
Yuki
Pomo
Wintun
Miwok
Costanoan
Yokuts
Salinan
Chumash

Carrier
Chilcotin
Shuswap
Lillooet
Thompson
Okanagan
Sanpoil
Colville
Spokane
Palouse
Walla Walla
Klamath
Modoc
Chomawi
Tsugewi
Kawaiisu
Mono
Panamint

Cayuse

Kaigani
Piegan
Kutenai
Kalispel
Atsina
Coeur D'Alene
Flathead
Crow
Nez Perce
Bannock
Shoshoni
Paviotso
Washo
N. Paiute
S. Paiute
Ute
Gosiute

Sarsi
Siksika (Blackfoot)
Cree

Hidatsa
Mandan
Arikara
Teton
Dakota
Ponca
Pawnee
N.Cheyenne
Arapaho
S.Cheyenne
Osage
Jicarilla Apache
Kiowa
Pueblo
Kiowa Apache
Mescalero Apache

Ojibwa (Chippewa)
Ottawa
Plains Cree
Assiniboin
Winnebago

Yankton
Dakota
Sauk
Fox
Iowa
Omaha
Oto
Kansa
Missouri
Quapaw

Naskapi Montagnais
Micmac
Malecite
Passamaquoddy
Penobscot
Abnaki
Huron

Tobacco
Neutral

Santee Dakota

Menomini

Erie

Kickapoo
Miami
Wea
Peoria
Illinois
Shawnee
Cherokee

Beothuk

Pennacook
Mahican
Mohawk
Nipmuc Oneida
Massachuset
Wampanoag
Narraganset
Pequot
Mohegan
Wappinger
Onondaga
Cayuga
Seneca
Delaware
Nanticoke
Powhatan
Chickahominy
Mattapony
Tutelo
Pamlico
Nottoway
Tuscarora
Catawba

Susquehanna
Pamunkey
Piankashaw
Potawatomie
Tuskegee
Yuchi

Mohave
Serrano
Yavapai
Cahuilla
Yuma
Pima
Maricopa
Papago

Cochimi

Kavasupai
Chemehuevi
Walapai

Navaho
Hopi
Zuni
W. Apache
Lipan Apache

Comanche
Kichai
Waco
Tonkawa

Tawakoni
Wichita
Caddo Natchez
Tunica

Choctaw Creek
Alabama
Chickasaw

Seminole

Opata
Seri
Tarahumara
Cahita
Acaxee

Concho
Coahuiltec
Tamaulipec
Huichol

Karankawa

Atakapa
Chitimacha
Biloxi
Mobile
Apalachee

Yamasee
Guale
Timucua
Hichiti

Calusa

Taino

Walcuri
Pericu
Yaqui

Toltec
Tarascan
Otomi

Huastec
Totonac
Tlaxcalan
Aztec
Mixtec

Coahuiltec

Yucatan Maya

Zapotec

Lacandon
Maya
Quiche
Maya

Ciboney

Mosquito

Chontal

0   600
Miles

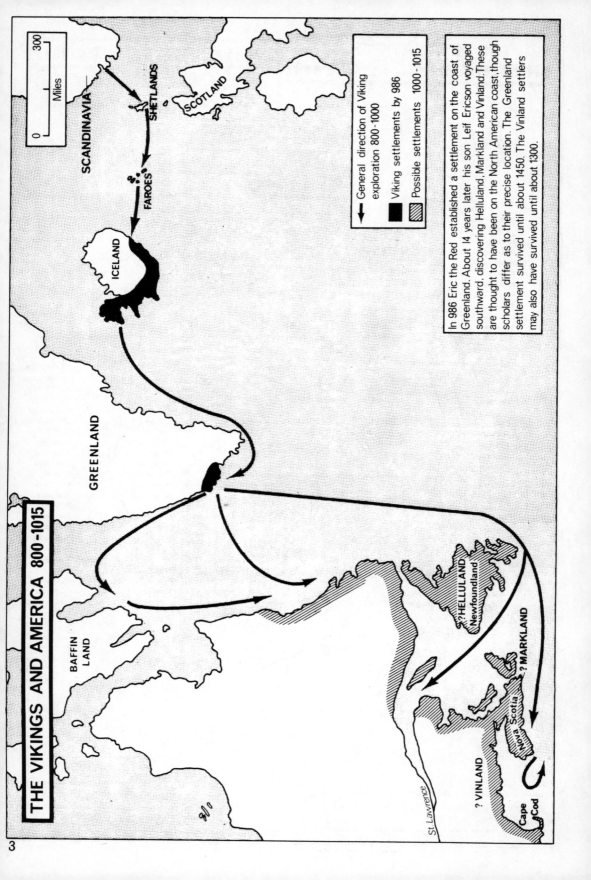

THE VIKINGS AND AMERICA 800-1015

SCANDINAVIA

SHETLANDS

SCOTLAND

FAROES

ICELAND

GREENLAND

BAFFIN LAND

St. Lawrence

?HELLULAND

Newfoundland

?MARKLAND

Nova Scotia

? VINLAND

Cape Cod

0   300
|————|————|
      Miles

General direction of Viking exploration 800-1000

Viking settlements by 986

Possible settlements 1000-1015

In 986 Eric the Red established a settlement on the coast of Greenland. About 14 years later his son Leif Ericson voyaged southward, discovering Helluland, Markland and Vinland. These are thought to have been on the North American coast, though scholars differ as to their precise location. The Greenland settlement survived until about 1450. The Vinland settlers may also have survived until about 1300.

3

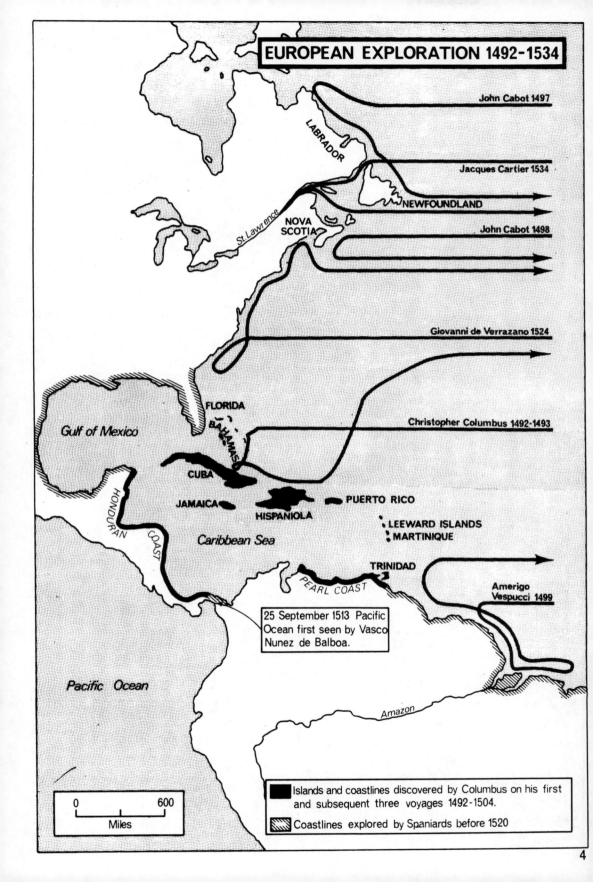

EUROPEAN EXPLORATION 1492-1534

John Cabot 1497

LABRADOR

Jacques Cartier 1534

NEWFOUNDLAND

John Cabot 1498

St. Lawrence

NOVA SCOTIA

Giovanni de Verrazano 1524

FLORIDA

Gulf of Mexico

BAHAMAS

Christopher Columbus 1492-1493

CUBA

JAMAICA

HISPANIOLA

PUERTO RICO

HONDURAN COAST

LEEWARD ISLANDS

MARTINIQUE

Caribbean Sea

TRINIDAD

PEARL COAST

Amerigo Vespucci 1499

25 September 1513 Pacific Ocean first seen by Vasco Nunez de Balboa.

Pacific Ocean

Amazon

0   600
Miles

■ Islands and coastlines discovered by Columbus on his first and subsequent three voyages 1492-1504.

▨ Coastlines explored by Spaniards before 1520

4

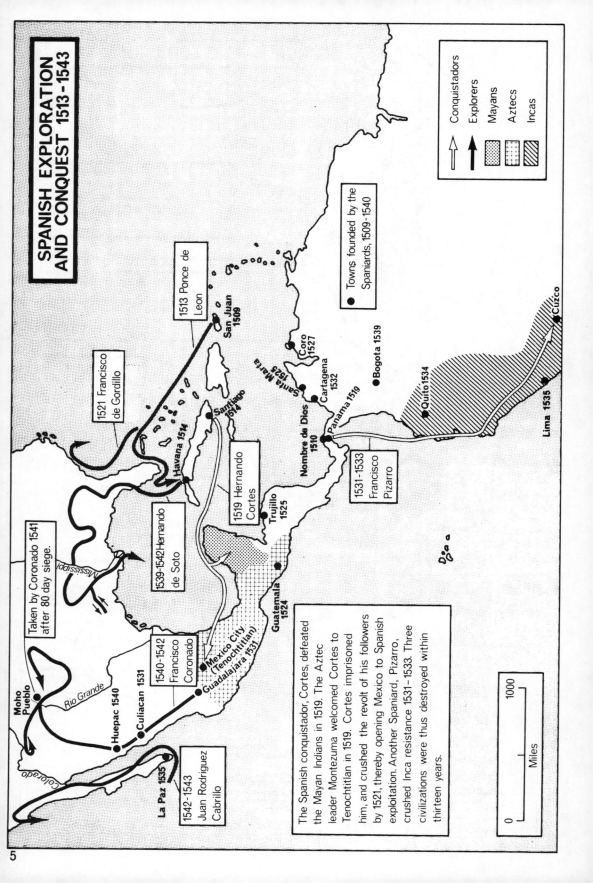

SPANISH EXPLORATION AND CONQUEST 1513-1543

Legend:
- Conquistadors
- Explorers
- Mayans
- Aztecs
- Incas

● Towns founded by the Spaniards, 1509-1540

1513 Ponce de Leon

1521 Francisco de Gordillo

1539-1542 Hernando de Soto

1519 Hernando Cortes

1531-1533 Francisco Pizarro

1540-1542 Francisco Coronado

1542-1543 Juan Rodriguez Cabrillo

Taken by Coronado 1541 after 80 day siege.

Moho Pueblo

Huepac 1540

Culiacan 1531

Rio Grande

Colorado

La Paz 1535

Mississippi

Mexico City (Tenochtitlan)

Guadalajara 1531

Guatemala 1524

San Juan 1509

Havana 1514

Santiago 1514

Trujillo 1525

Coro 1527

Santa Marta 1525

Cartagena 1532

Nombre de Dios 1510

Panama 1519

Bogota 1539

Quito 1534

Lima 1535

Cuzco

The Spanish conquistador, Cortes, defeated the Mayan Indians in 1519. The Aztec leader Montezuma welcomed Cortes to Tenochtitlan in 1519. Cortes imprisoned him, and crushed the revolt of his followers by 1521, thereby opening Mexico to Spanish exploitation. Another Spaniard, Pizarro, crushed Inca resistance 1531-1533. Three civilizations were thus destroyed within thirteen years.

Miles

0   1000

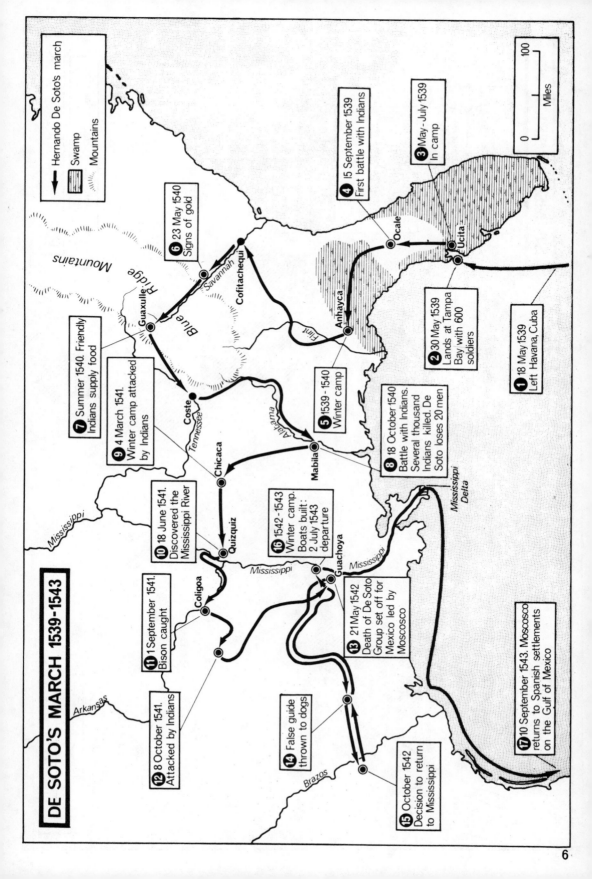

DE SOTO'S MARCH 1539-1543

Key:
- Hernando De Soto's march
- Swamp
- Mountains

0 ___ 100 Miles

1 18 May 1539 Left Havana, Cuba

2 30 May 1539 Lands at Tampa Bay with 600 soldiers

3 May - July 1539 In camp

4 15 September 1539 First battle with Indians

5 1539 - 1540 Winter camp

6 23 May 1540 Signs of gold

7 Summer 1540. Friendly Indians supply food

8 18 October 1540 Battle with Indians. Several thousand Indians killed. De Soto loses 20 men

9 4 March 1541. Winter camp attacked by Indians

10 18 June 1541. Discovered the Mississippi River

11 1 September 1541. Bison caught

12 8 October 1541. Attacked by Indians

13 21 May 1542 Death of De Soto Group set off for Mexico led by Moscosco

14 False guide thrown to dogs

15 October 1542 Decision to return to Mississippi

16 1542 -1543 Winter camp. Boats built: 2 July 1543 departure

17 10 September 1543. Moscosco returns to Spanish settlements on the Gulf of Mexico

Ucita, Ocale, Anhayca, Cofitachequi, Savannah, Guaxulle, Coste, Chicaca, Quizquiz, Coligoa, Mabila, Guachoya

Blue Ridge Mountains, Mountains

Flint, Alatama, Tennessee, Mississippi, Arkansas, Brazos, Mississippi Delta

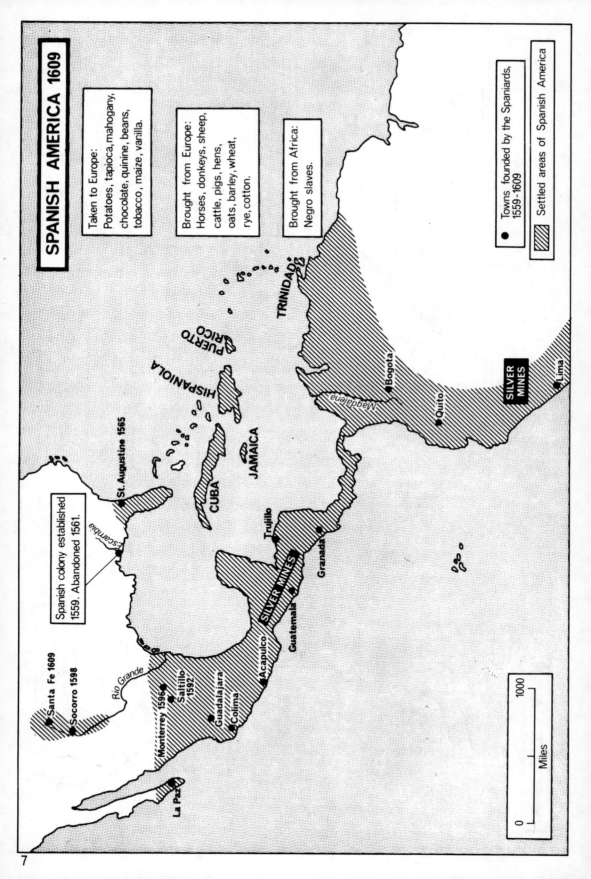

SPANISH AMERICA 1609

Taken to Europe:
Potatoes, tapioca, mahogany, chocolate, quinine, beans, tobacco, maize, vanilla.

Brought from Europe:
Horses, donkeys, sheep, cattle, pigs, hens, oats, barley, wheat, rye, cotton.

Brought from Africa:
Negro slaves.

● Towns founded by the Spaniards, 1559 -1609

▨ Settled areas of Spanish America

Spanish colony established 1559. Abandoned 1561.

Escambia

Rio Grande

St. Augustine 1565

Santa Fe 1609
Socorro 1598

Monterrey 1596
Saltillo 1592
Guadalajara
Colima
Acapulco

La Paz

SILVER MINES

Guatemala
Granada
Trujillo

CUBA
JAMAICA
HISPANIOLA
PUERTO RICO
TRINIDAD

Magdalena

Bogota
Quito

SILVER MINES
Lima

Miles

0   1000

7

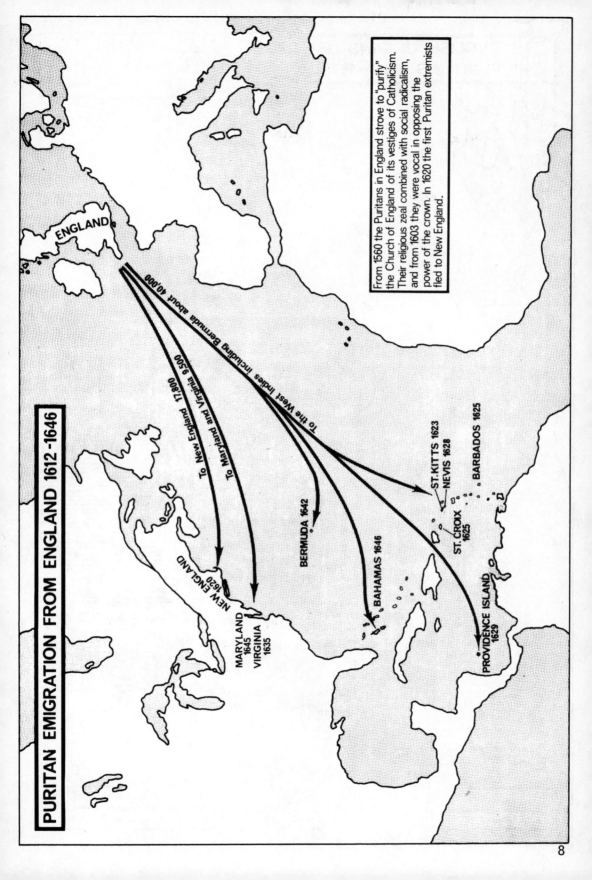

PURITAN EMIGRATION FROM ENGLAND 1612 -1646

ENGLAND

From 1560 the Puritans in England strove to "purify" the Church of England of its vestiges of Catholicism. Their religious zeal combined with social radicalism, and from 1603 they were vocal in opposing the power of the crown. In 1620 the first Puritan extremists fled to New England.

To the West Indies including Bermuda about 40,000

To Maryland and Virginia 9,500

To New England and Virginia 17,800

NEW ENGLAND 1620

MARYLAND 1645
VIRGINIA 1635

BERMUDA 1642

BAHAMAS 1646

ST. KITTS 1623
NEVIS 1628

ST. CROIX 1625

BARBADOS 1625

PROVIDENCE ISLAND 1629

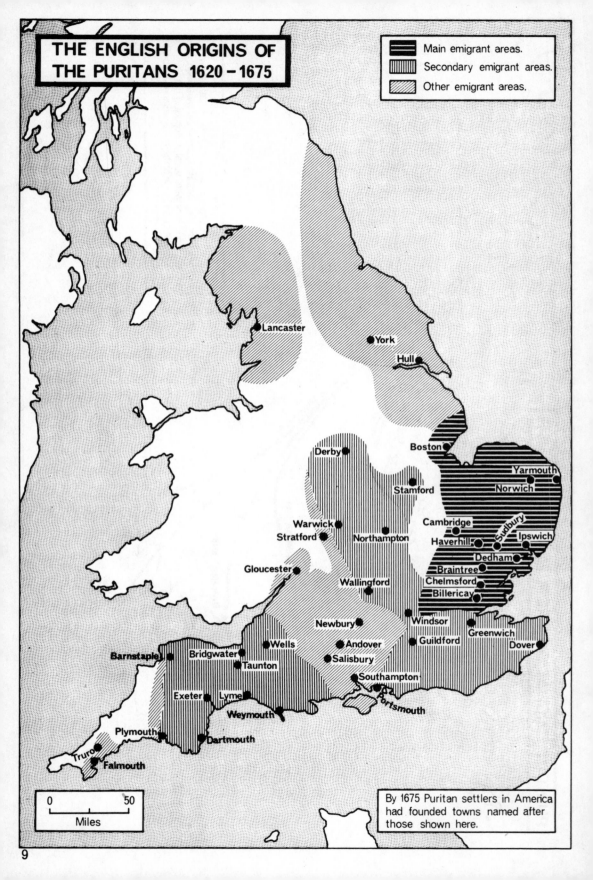

THE ENGLISH ORIGINS OF THE PURITANS 1620 – 1675

Main emigrant areas.
Secondary emigrant areas.
Other emigrant areas.

Lancaster

York

Hull

Derby

Boston

Yarmouth

Stamford

Norwich

Warwick

Cambridge

Sudbury

Stratford

Northampton

Haverhill

Ipswich

Gloucester

Dedham

Braintree

Wallingford

Chelmsford

Billericay

Newbury

Windsor

Greenwich

Andover

Guildford

Dover

Barnstaple

Bridgwater

Wells

Salisbury

Taunton

Southampton

Exeter

Lyme

Portsmouth

Weymouth

Plymouth

Dartmouth

Truro

Falmouth

0   50
Miles

By 1675 Puritan settlers in America had founded towns named after those shown here.

9

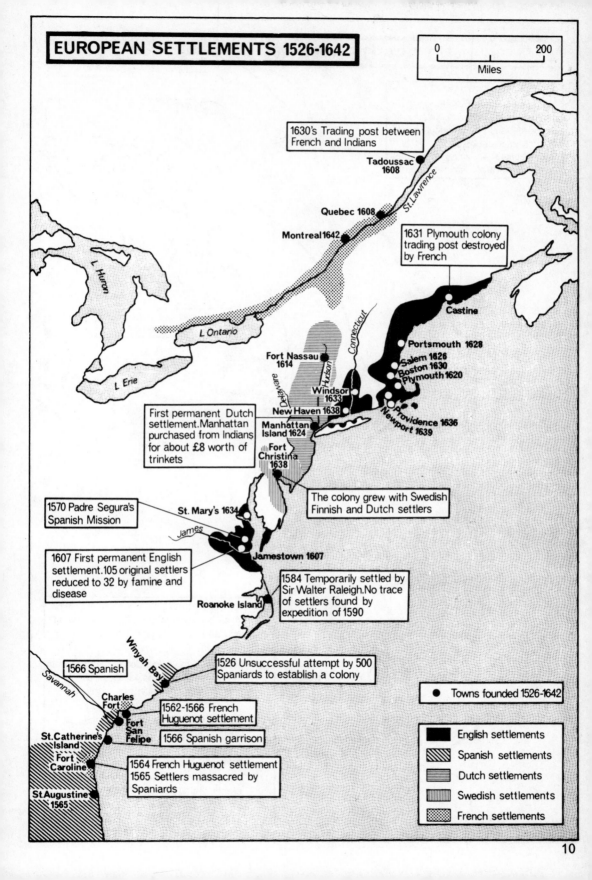

EUROPEAN SETTLEMENTS 1526-1642

0   200
Miles

1630's Trading post between French and Indians

Tadoussac 1608

Quebec 1608

St. Lawrence

Montreal 1642

1631 Plymouth colony trading post destroyed by French

L. Huron

L. Ontario

L. Erie

Castine

Portsmouth 1628

Fort Nassau 1614

Connecticut

Salem 1626
Boston 1630
Plymouth 1620

Windsor 1633

Delaware

Hudson

New Haven 1638

Providence 1636
Newport 1639

First permanent Dutch settlement. Manhattan purchased from Indians for about £8 worth of trinkets

Manhattan Island 1624

Fort Christina 1638

The colony grew with Swedish Finnish and Dutch settlers

1570 Padre Segura's Spanish Mission

St. Mary's 1634

James

1607 First permanent English settlement. 105 original settlers reduced to 32 by famine and disease

Jamestown 1607

1584 Temporarily settled by Sir Walter Raleigh. No trace of settlers found by expedition of 1590

Roanoke Island

Winyah Bay

1526 Unsuccessful attempt by 500 Spaniards to establish a colony

Savannah

1566 Spanish

Charles Fort

1562-1566 French Huguenot settlement

Fort San Felipe

1566 Spanish garrison

St. Catherine's Island

Fort Caroline

1564 French Huguenot settlement
1565 Settlers massacred by Spaniards

St. Augustine 1565

● Towns founded 1526-1642

■ English settlements
▨ Spanish settlements
▤ Dutch settlements
▥ Swedish settlements
▦ French settlements

10

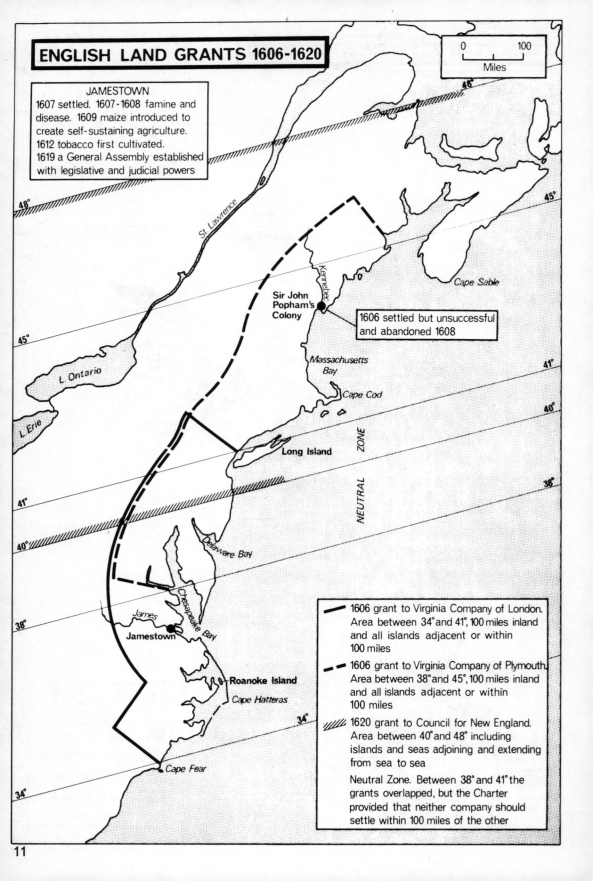

ENGLISH LAND GRANTS 1606-1620

0   100
Miles

JAMESTOWN
1607 settled. 1607-1608 famine and
disease. 1609 maize introduced to
create self-sustaining agriculture.
1612 tobacco first cultivated.
1619 a General Assembly established
with legislative and judicial powers

St. Lawrence

Cape Sable

Kennebec

**Sir John
Popham's
Colony**

1606 settled but unsuccessful
and abandoned 1608

Massachusetts
Bay

Cape Cod

L. Ontario

L. Erie

NEUTRAL ZONE

Long Island

Delaware Bay

Chesapeake Bay

James

Jamestown

Roanoke Island

Cape Hatteras

Cape Fear

1606 grant to Virginia Company of London.
Area between 34° and 41°, 100 miles inland
and all islands adjacent or within
100 miles

1606 grant to Virginia Company of Plymouth.
Area between 38° and 45°, 100 miles inland
and all islands adjacent or within
100 miles

1620 grant to Council for New England.
Area between 40° and 48° including
islands and seas adjoining and extending
from sea to sea

Neutral Zone. Between 38° and 41° the
grants overlapped, but the Charter
provided that neither company should
settle within 100 miles of the other

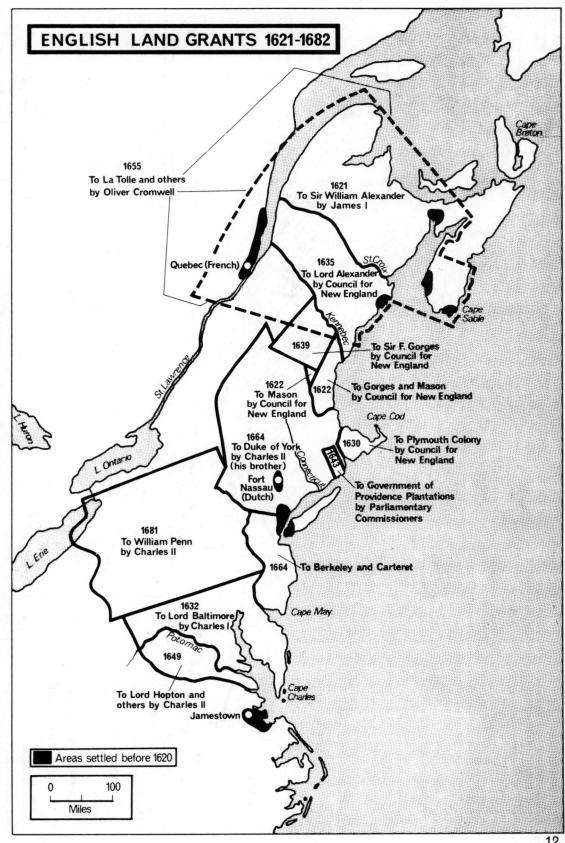

ENGLISH LAND GRANTS 1621-1682

1655
To La Tolle and others
by Oliver Cromwell

1621
To Sir William Alexander
by James I

Quebec (French)

1635
To Lord Alexander
by Council for
New England

St Croix

Kennebec

1639

To Sir F. Gorges
by Council for
New England

1622
To Mason
by Council for
New England

1622

To Gorges and Mason
by Council for New England

Cape Cod

Cape Breton

Cape Sable

1664
To Duke of York
by Charles II
(his brother)

1630

To Plymouth Colony
by Council for
New England

Fort
Nassau
(Dutch)

Connecticut

1643

To Government of
Providence Plantations
by Parliamentary
Commissioners

Huron

L. Ontario

L. Erie

1681
To William Penn
by Charles II

1664 ⟶ To Berkeley and Carteret

1632
To Lord Baltimore
by Charles I

Cape May

Potomac

1649

St Lawrence

To Lord Hopton and
others by Charles II
Jamestown

Cape Charles

	Areas settled before 1620

```
0          100
|_____|
   Miles
```

12

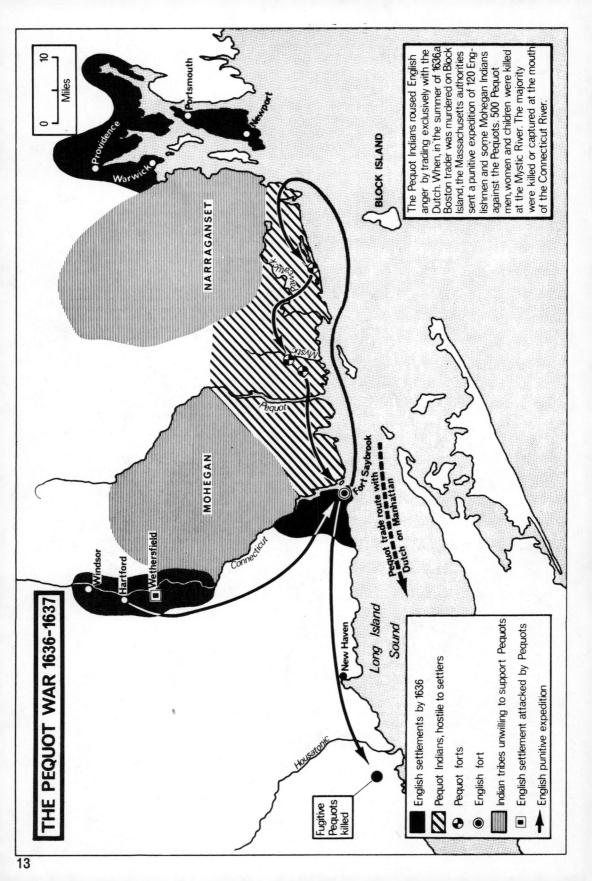

THE PEQUOT WAR 1636-1637

The Pequot Indians roused English anger by trading exclusively with the Dutch. When, in the summer of 1636, a Boston trader was murdered on Block Island, the Massachusetts authorities sent a punitive expedition of 120 Englishmen and some Mohegan Indians against the Pequots. 500 Pequot men, women and children were killed at the Mystic River. The majority were killed or captured at the mouth of the Connecticut River.

Miles
0   10

Providence
Warwick
Portsmouth
Newport

NARRAGANSET

BLOCK ISLAND

MOHEGAN

Pawcatuck
Mystic
Pequot

Windsor
Hartford
Wethersfield
Connecticut

Fort Saybrook

Pequot trade route with Dutch on Manhattan

New Haven

Long Island Sound

Housatonic

Fugitive Pequots killed

■ English settlements by 1636

▨ Pequot Indians, hostile to settlers

⊕ Pequot forts

◉ English fort

▦ Indian tribes unwilling to support Pequots

▣ English settlement attacked by Pequots

↑ English punitive expedition

13

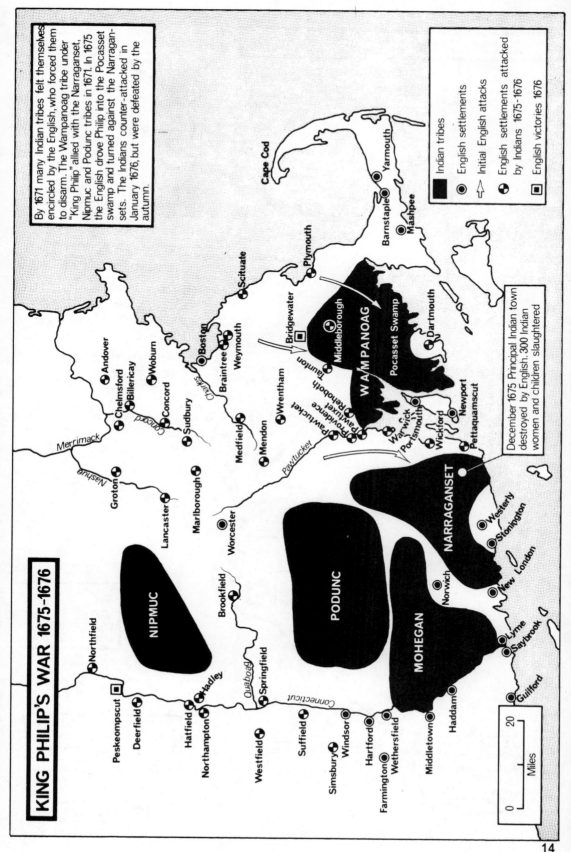

KING PHILIP'S WAR 1675-1676

By 1671 many Indian tribes felt themselves encircled by the English, who forced them to disarm. The Wampanoag tribe under "King Philip" allied with the Narraganset, Nipmuc and Podunc tribes in 1671. In 1675 the English drove Philip into the Pocasset swamp and turned against the Narragansets. The Indians counter-attacked in January 1676, but were defeated by the autumn.

Indian tribes

English settlements

Initial English attacks

English settlements attacked by Indians 1675-1676

English victories 1676

December 1675 Principal Indian town destroyed by English. 300 Indian women and children slaughtered

Miles

0   20

Cape Cod

Yarmouth

Barnstaple

Mashpee

Plymouth

Scituate

Bridgewater

Middleborough

WAMPANOAG

Pocasset Swamp

Dartmouth

Boston

Braintree

Weymouth

Wrentham

Taunton

Rehoboth

Newport

Pettaquamscut

Pawtucket

Providence

Warwick

Portsmouth

Wickford

Andover

Chelmsford

Billericay

Woburn

Concord

Sudbury

Medfield

Mendon

Charles

Concord

Merrimack

Groton

Marlborough

Worcester

Lancaster

Nashua

Pawtucker

Westerly

Stonington

NARRAGANSET

New London

Norwich

PODUNC

MOHEGAN

Lyme

Saybrook

Guilford

Haddam

Middletown

Wethersfield

Hartford

Farmington

Windsor

Simsbury

Suffield

Westfield

Northampton

Hatfield

Hadley

Deerfield

Peskeompscut

Northfield

NIPMUC

Brookfield

Springfield

Quaboag

Connecticut

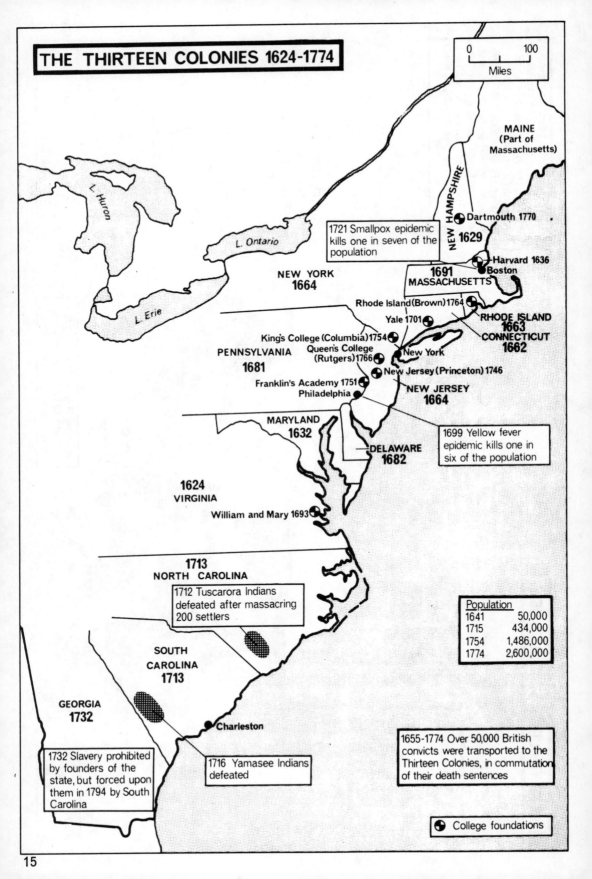

THE THIRTEEN COLONIES 1624-1774

0   100
Miles

L. Huron

L. Ontario

L. Erie

MAINE
(Part of
Massachusetts)

NEW HAMPSHIRE
1629

● Dartmouth 1770

1721 Smallpox epidemic
kills one in seven of the
population

NEW YORK
1664

Harvard 1636
Boston

1691
MASSACHUSETTS

Rhode Island (Brown) 1764

Yale 1701

RHODE ISLAND
1663
CONNECTICUT
1662

King's College (Columbia) 1754

Queen's College
(Rutgers) 1766

New York

PENNSYLVANIA
1681

New Jersey (Princeton) 1746

Franklin's Academy 1751

Philadelphia

NEW JERSEY
1664

MARYLAND
1632

DELAWARE
1682

1699 Yellow fever
epidemic kills one in
six of the population

1624
VIRGINIA

William and Mary 1693

1713
NORTH CAROLINA

1712 Tuscarora Indians
defeated after massacring
200 settlers

Population
1641   50,000
1715   434,000
1754   1,486,000
1774   2,600,000

SOUTH
CAROLINA
1713

GEORGIA
1732

● Charleston

1732 Slavery prohibited
by founders of the
state, but forced upon
them in 1794 by South
Carolina

1716 Yamasee Indians
defeated

1655-1774 Over 50,000 British
convicts were transported to the
Thirteen Colonies, in commutation
of their death sentences

⊕ College foundations

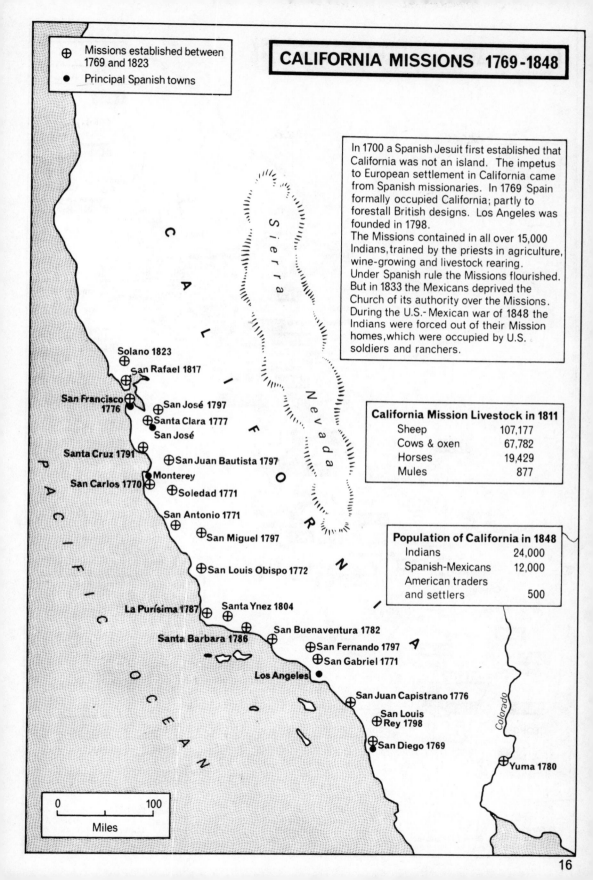

CALIFORNIA MISSIONS 1769-1848

⊕ Missions established between 1769 and 1823

● Principal Spanish towns

In 1700 a Spanish Jesuit first established that California was not an island. The impetus to European settlement in California came from Spanish missionaries. In 1769 Spain formally occupied California; partly to forestall British designs. Los Angeles was founded in 1798.
The Missions contained in all over 15,000 Indians, trained by the priests in agriculture, wine-growing and livestock rearing.
Under Spanish rule the Missions flourished. But in 1833 the Mexicans deprived the Church of its authority over the Missions. During the U.S.- Mexican war of 1848 the Indians were forced out of their Mission homes, which were occupied by U.S. soldiers and ranchers.

California Mission Livestock in 1811

Sheep	107,177
Cows & oxen	67,782
Horses	19,429
Mules	877

Population of California in 1848

Indians	24,000
Spanish-Mexicans	12,000
American traders and settlers	500

Sierra Nevada

C A L I F O R N I A

PACIFIC OCEAN

Colorado

Solano 1823
San Rafael 1817
San Francisco 1776
San José 1797
Santa Clara 1777
San José
Santa Cruz 1791
San Juan Bautista 1797
Monterey
San Carlos 1770
Soledad 1771
San Antonio 1771
San Miguel 1797
San Louis Obispo 1772
La Purísima 1787
Santa Ynez 1804
Santa Barbara 1786
San Buenaventura 1782
San Fernando 1797
San Gabriel 1771
Los Angeles
San Juan Capistrano 1776
San Louis Rey 1798
San Diego 1769
Yuma 1780

0   100
Miles

16

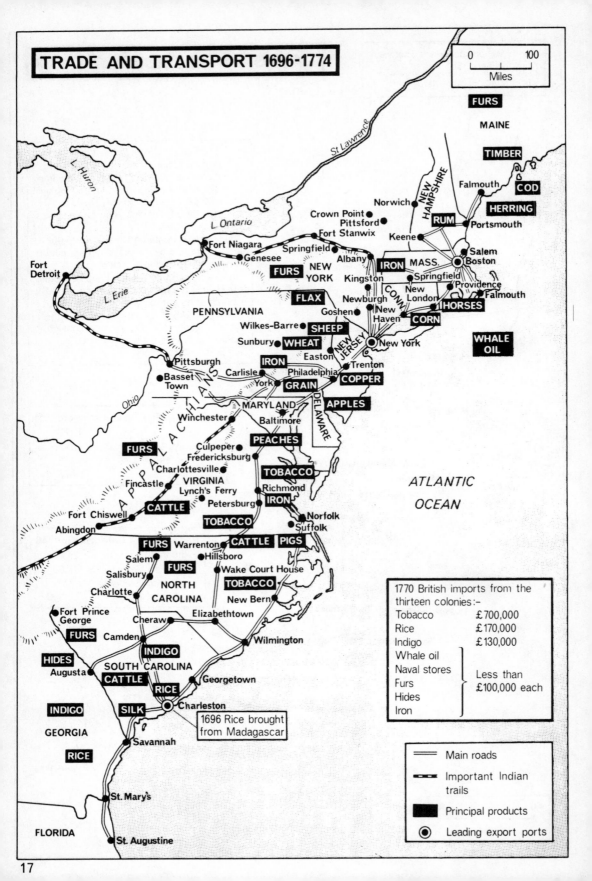

TRADE AND TRANSPORT 1696-1774

0   100
Miles

MAINE

FURS

TIMBER

Falmouth

COD

HERRING

Portsmouth

St Lawrence

NEW HAMPSHIRE

Norwich

Crown Point

Pittsford

Fort Stanwix

Keene

RUM

IRON

Salem

Boston

MASS.

L. Ontario

Fort Niagara

Springfield

Genesee

Albany

Kingston

Springfield

New London

Providence

Falmouth

L. Huron

FURS

NEW YORK

Newburgh

Goshen

New Haven

CORN

CONN.

HORSES

Fort Detroit

FLAX

PENNSYLVANIA

Wilkes-Barre

SHEEP

Sunbury

WHEAT

Easton

New York

WHALE OIL

L. Erie

NEW JERSEY

Trenton

Pittsburgh

IRON

Carlisle

Philadelphia

COPPER

Basset Town

York

GRAIN

Ohio

MARYLAND

DELAWARE

APPLES

Winchester

Baltimore

Culpeper

PEACHES

FURS

Fredericksburg

Charlottesville

TOBACCO

Fincastle

VIRGINIA

Lynch's Ferry

Richmond

Petersburg

IRON

Fort Chiswell

CATTLE

Abingdon

TOBACCO

Norfolk

Suffolk

FURS

Warrenton

CATTLE

PIGS

Salem

Hillsboro

Salisbury

FURS

Wake Court House

Charlotte

NORTH CAROLINA

TOBACCO

Fort Prince George

New Bern

Cheraw

Elizabethtown

FURS

Camden

Wilmington

INDIGO

HIDES

SOUTH CAROLINA

Augusta

CATTLE

Georgetown

RICE

INDIGO

SILK

Charleston

GEORGIA

1696 Rice brought from Madagascar

RICE

Savannah

St. Mary's

FLORIDA

St. Augustine

ATLANTIC OCEAN

1770 British imports from the thirteen colonies:-
Tobacco   £700,000
Rice   £170,000
Indigo   £130,000
Whale oil
Naval stores
Furs   } Less than
Hides   } £100,000 each
Iron

───── Main roads

■-■-■ Important Indian trails

■ Principal products

◉ Leading export ports

17

QUEEN ANNE'S WAR 1702-1713

The American part of the War of the Spanish Succession

1710 English naval attack on Quebec wrecked in fog.

Bonavista Captured 1704
St.John's Captured 1708
Placentia
NEWFOUNDLAND

Hudson Bay

St. Lawrence

F R E N C H
C A N A D A

Quebec

ACADIA
Port Royal Captured 1710

NOVA SCOTIA

Winter Harbour

Montreal

Wells

Fort Frontenac

Fort Niagara

Albany   **Deerfield**

Fort Pontchartrain

New York

1710 English naval attacks.

Fort St.Joseph

APPALACHIANS

In 1702 England joined the Grand Alliance in Europe against France and Spain. In the American south, English troops, allied with Indians, destroyed 13 of the 14 Spanish missions, but failed to destroy the French forts. In the north the French and Indians combined. By the Treaty of Utrecht, 1713, France surrendered Newfoundland, Acadia and the Hudson Bay area to the English.

Fort Prudhomme
CHICKASAW
Fort Tombecbé
CREEKS
Mississippi
YAZOO   **ALABAMA**

Fort Maurepas
Fort Mobile
Pensacola

San Marcos

St. Augustine Fort besieged town burned

■	English possessions
→	English attacks 1702-1703.
◑	Spanish missions destroyed by the English 1703.
░	Indian tribes won over by English bribes 1703-1706.
▦	Choctaw tribe remaining loyal to France.
◉	French forts.
⇨	French and Indian attacks 1703-1709.

0   300
Miles

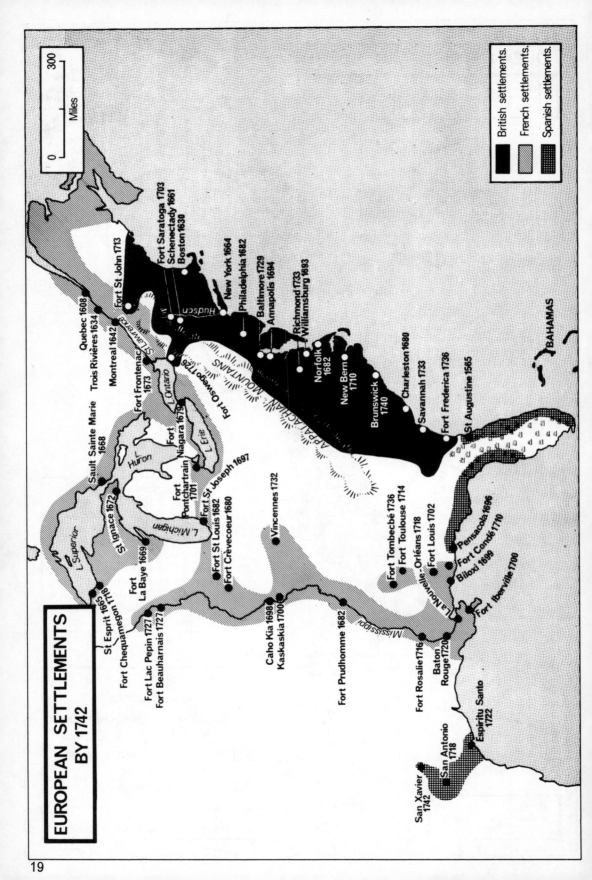

EUROPEAN SETTLEMENTS BY 1742

300
Miles
0

British settlements.
French settlements.
Spanish settlements.

Quebec 1608
Trois Rivières 1634
Montreal 1642
Fort St John 1713
Fort Saratoga 1703
Schenectady 1661
Boston 1630
New York 1664
Philadelphia 1682
Baltimore 1729
Annapolis 1694
Richmond 1733
Williamsburg 1693
Norfolk 1682
New Bern 1710
Brunswick 1740
Charleston 1680
Savannah 1733
Fort Frederica f 1736
St Augustine 1565
BAHAMAS

St. Lawrence
Hudson
L. Ontario
L. Erie
APPALACHIAN MOUNTAINS

Sault Sainte Marie 1668
Fort Frontenac 1673
Fort Oswego 1726
Fort Niagara 1679
Fort Pontchartrain 1701
Fort St Joseph 1697
L Huron
L. Michigan
St Ignace 1672
Fort St Louis 1682
Fort Crèvecoeur 1680
Vincennes 1732
Fort Tombecbé 1736
Fort Toulouse 1714
Fort Louis 1702
Pensacola 1696
Fort Condé 1710
Biloxi 1699
Fort Iberville 1700
La Nouvelle-Orléans 1718

L. Superior
St Esprit 1665
Fort Chequamegon 1718
Fort Lac Pepin 1727
Fort Beauharnais 1727
Fort La Baye 1669
Caho Kia 1698
Kaskaskia 1700
Fort Prudhomme 1682
Fort Rosalie 1716
Baton Rouge 1720
Espiritu Santo 1722
San Antonio 1718
San Xavier 1742
Mississippi

19

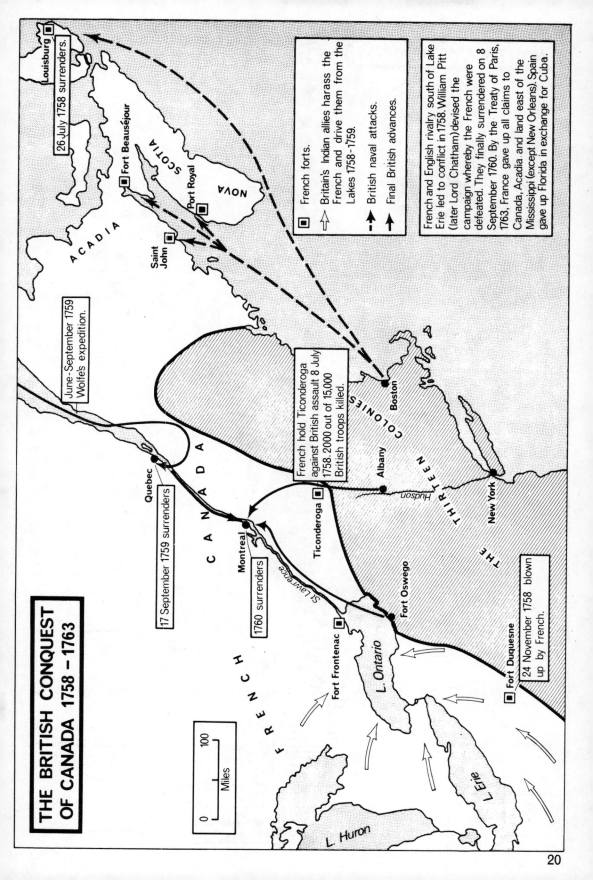

THE BRITISH CONQUEST OF CANADA 1758 – 1763

Key:

■ French forts.

⇨ Britain's Indian allies harass the French and drive them from the Lakes 1758-1759.

◄┄ British naval attacks.

◄━ Final British advances.

French and English rivalry south of Lake Erie led to conflict in 1758. William Pitt (later Lord Chatham) devised the campaign whereby the French were defeated. They finally surrendered on 8 September 1760. By the Treaty of Paris, 1763, France gave up all claims to Canada, Acadia, and land east of the Mississippi (except New Orleans). Spain gave up Florida in exchange for Cuba.

Louisburg — 26 July 1758 surrenders.

June-September 1759 Wolfe's expedition.

French hold Ticonderoga against British assault 8 July 1758. 2000 out of 15,000 British troops killed.

Quebec — 17 September 1759 surrenders

Montreal — 1760 surrenders

24 November 1758 blown up by French.

Fort Beauséjour

Port Royal

Saint John

ACADIA

NOVA SCOTIA

CANADA

FRENCH

Ticonderoga

Albany

Hudson

Boston

New York

THE THIRTEEN COLONIES

Fort Oswego

L. Ontario

Fort Frontenac

Fort Duquesne

L. Erie

L. Huron

St Lawrence

Miles
0   100

20

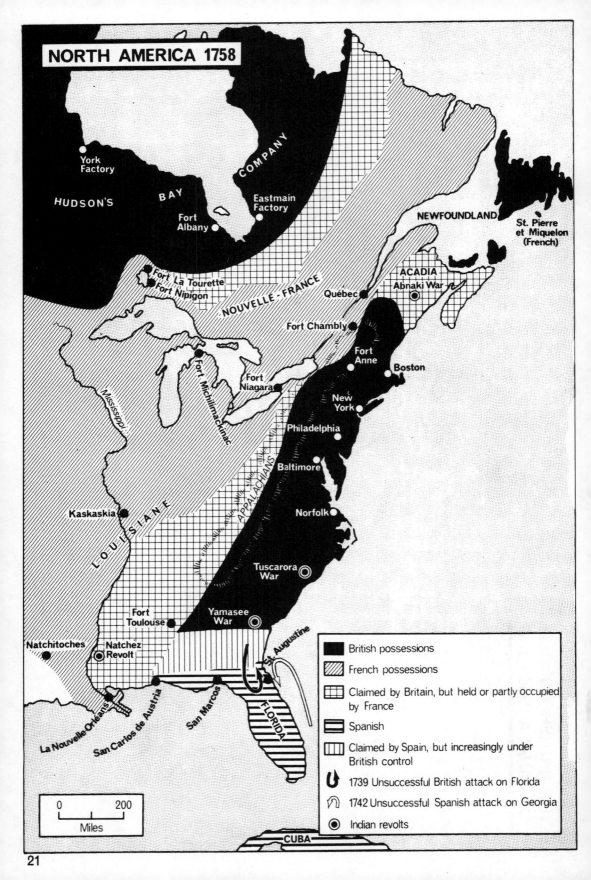

NORTH AMERICA 1758

York
Factory

HUDSON'S   BAY   COMPANY

Fort
Albany

Eastmain
Factory

NEWFOUNDLAND

St. Pierre
et Miquelon
(French)

Fort La Tourette
Fort Nipigon

NOUVELLE-FRANCE

Québec

ACADIA
Abnaki War

Fort Chambly

Fort
Anne

Boston

Fort
Michilimackinac

Fort
Niagara

New
York

Mississippi

Philadelphia

APPALACHIANS

Baltimore

Kaskaskia

Norfolk

L O U I S I A N E

Tuscarora
War

Fort
Toulouse

Yamasee
War

Natchitoches

Natchez
Revolt

St. Augustine

La Nouvelle-Orléans

San Carlos de Austria

San Marcos

FLORIDA

	British possessions
	French possessions
	Claimed by Britain, but held or partly occupied by France
	Spanish
	Claimed by Spain, but increasingly under British control
↵	1739 Unsuccessful British attack on Florida
↷	1742 Unsuccessful Spanish attack on Georgia
◉	Indian revolts

0   200
Miles

CUBA

21

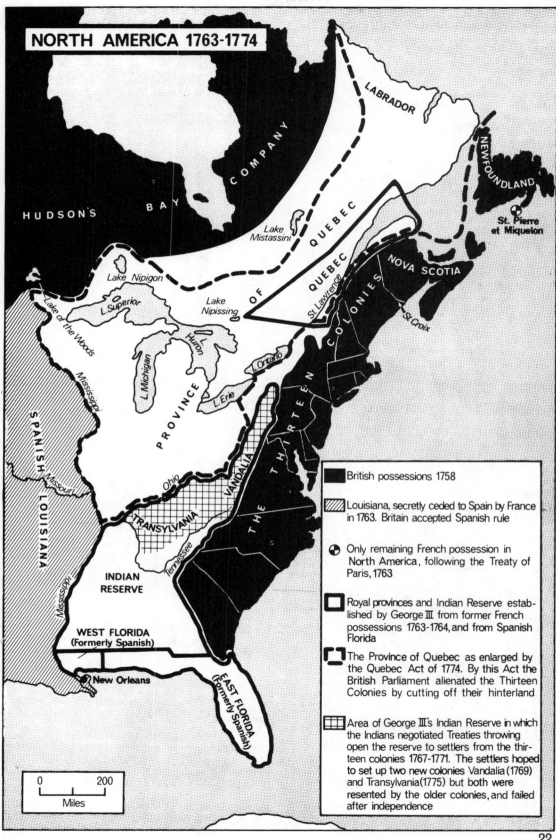

NORTH AMERICA 1763-1774

HUDSON'S BAY COMPANY

LABRADOR

NEWFOUNDLAND

St. Pierre et Miquelon

Lake Mistassini

PROVINCE OF QUEBEC

NOVA SCOTIA

St Lawrence

St Croix

Lake Nipigon

Lake Nipissing

L. Superior

Lake of the Woods

L. Huron

L. Michigan

L. Ontario

L. Erie

Mississippi

SPANISH LOUISIANA

Missouri

Ohio

VANDALIA

THE THIRTEEN COLONIES

TRANSYLVANIA

Tennessee

INDIAN RESERVE

Mississippi

WEST FLORIDA (Formerly Spanish)

New Orleans

EAST FLORIDA (Formerly Spanish)

0   200
Miles

■ British possessions 1758

▨ Louisiana, secretly ceded to Spain by France in 1763. Britain accepted Spanish rule

◑ Only remaining French possession in North America, following the Treaty of Paris, 1763

☐ Royal provinces and Indian Reserve established by George III from former French possessions 1763-1764, and from Spanish Florida

⌐⌐ The Province of Quebec as enlarged by the Quebec Act of 1774. By this Act the British Parliament alienated the Thirteen Colonies by cutting off their hinterland

▦ Area of George III's Indian Reserve in which the Indians negotiated Treaties throwing open the reserve to settlers from the thirteen colonies 1767-1771. The settlers hoped to set up two new colonies Vandalia (1769) and Transylvania (1775) but both were resented by the older colonies, and failed after independence

22

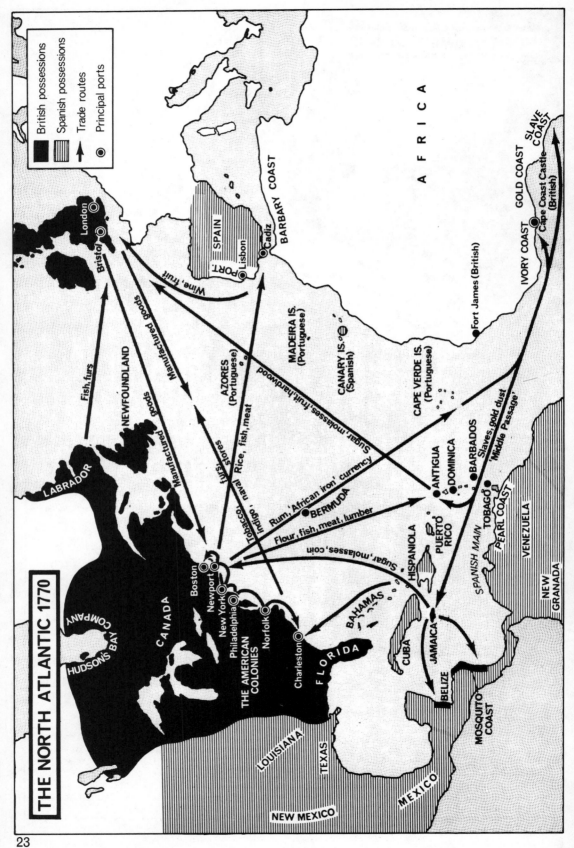

THE NORTH ATLANTIC 1770

British possessions
Spanish possessions
Trade routes
◎ Principal ports

LABRADOR

HUDSON'S BAY COMPANY

CANADA

NEWFOUNDLAND

Fish, furs

Manufactured goods

Manufactured goods

furs, stores

Tobacco, naval stores, Rice, fish, meat

THE AMERICAN COLONIES

Boston
Newport
New York
Philadelphia
Norfolk
Charleston

FLORIDA

LOUISIANA

TEXAS

NEW MEXICO

MEXICO

Indigo, naval stores, Rice, fish, meat

Rum, 'African iron' currency

BERMUDA

Flour, fish, meat, lumber

BAHAMAS

Sugar, molasses, coin

CUBA

HISPANIOLA

JAMAICA

BELIZE

MOSQUITO COAST

NEW GRANADA

VENEZUELA

PUERTO RICO

SPANISH MAIN

PEARL COAST

TOBAGO

DOMINICA

ANTIGUA

BARBADOS

Slaves, gold dust

'Middle Passage'

Sugar, molasses, fruit, hardwood

CAPE VERDE IS.
(Portuguese)

CANARY IS.
(Spanish)

MADEIRA IS.
(Portuguese)

AZORES
(Portuguese)

Wine, fruit

PORT.
Lisbon

SPAIN
Cadiz

London
Bristol

BARBARY COAST

A F R I C A

IVORY COAST

GOLD COAST

SLAVE COAST

Cape Coast Castle (British)

Fort James (British)

23

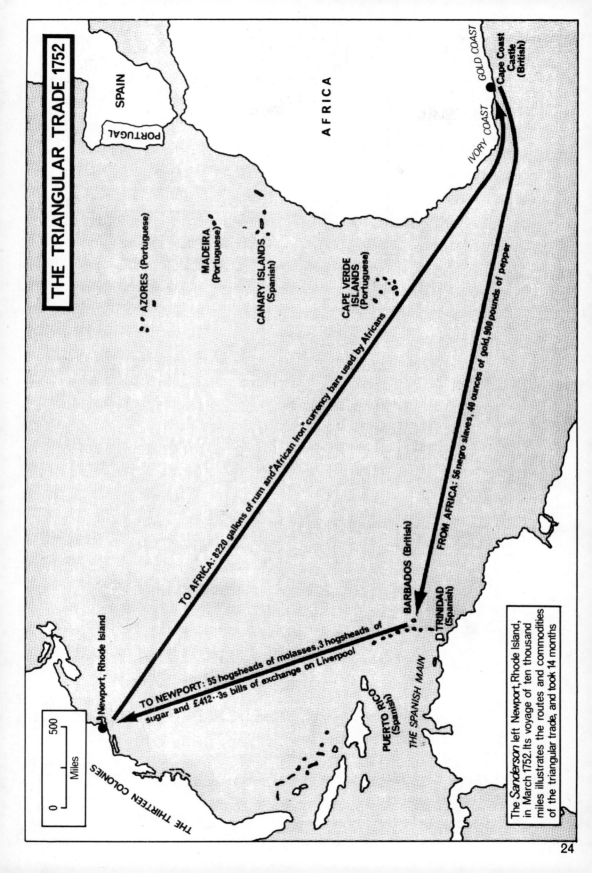

THE TRIANGULAR TRADE 1752

SPAIN

PORTUGAL

AFRICA

GOLD COAST

Cape Coast Castle (British)

IVORY COAST

AZORES (Portuguese)

MADEIRA (Portuguese)

CANARY ISLANDS (Spanish)

CAPE VERDE ISLANDS (Portuguese)

TO AFRICA: 8220 gallons of rum and 'African iron' currency bars used by Africans

FROM AFRICA: 56 negro slaves, 40 ounces of gold, 900 pounds of pepper

Newport, Rhode Island

BARBADOS (British)

TRINIDAD (Spanish)

PUERTO RICO (Spanish)

THE SPANISH MAIN

TO NEWPORT: 55 hogsheads of molasses, 3 hogsheads of sugar and £412··3s bills of exchange on Liverpool

THE THIRTEEN COLONIES

500
0
Miles

The *Sanderson* left Newport, Rhode Island, in March 1752. Its voyage of ten thousand miles illustrates the routes and commodities of the triangular trade, and took 14 months

24

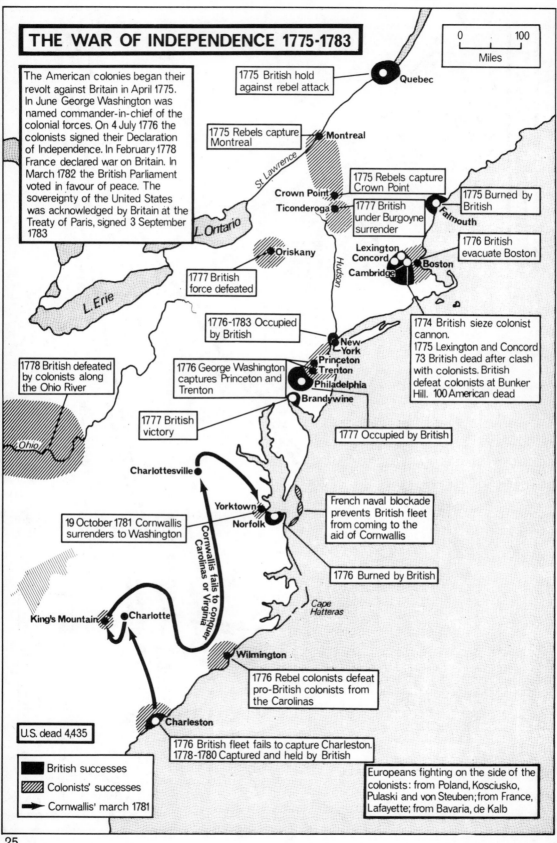

THE WAR OF INDEPENDENCE 1775-1783

0 ____ 100
Miles

The American colonies began their revolt against Britain in April 1775. In June George Washington was named commander-in-chief of the colonial forces. On 4 July 1776 the colonists signed their Declaration of Independence. In February 1778 France declared war on Britain. In March 1782 the British Parliament voted in favour of peace. The sovereignty of the United States was acknowledged by Britain at the Treaty of Paris, signed 3 September 1783

1775 British hold against rebel attack

Quebec

1775 Rebels capture Montreal

Montreal

St Lawrence

1775 Rebels capture Crown Point

Crown Point

Ticonderoga

1777 British under Burgoyne surrender

Falmouth

1775 Burned by British

1776 British evacuate Boston

L.Ontario

Hudson

Oriskany

1777 British force defeated

Lexington
Concord
Cambridge

Boston

L. Erie

1776-1783 Occupied by British

New York

1774 British sieze colonist cannon.
1775 Lexington and Concord 73 British dead after clash with colonists. British defeat colonists at Bunker Hill. 100 American dead

1778 British defeated by colonists along the Ohio River

1776 George Washington captures Princeton and Trenton

Princeton
Trenton
Philadelphia
Brandywine

Ohio

1777 British victory

1777 Occupied by British

Charlottesville

Yorktown
Norfolk

French naval blockade prevents British fleet from coming to the aid of Cornwallis

19 October 1781 Cornwallis surrenders to Washington

Cornwallis fails to conquer Carolinas or Virginia

1776 Burned by British

Cape Hatteras

King's Mountain

Charlotte

Wilmington

1776 Rebel colonists defeat pro-British colonists from the Carolinas

U.S. dead 4,435

Charleston

1776 British fleet fails to capture Charleston.
1778-1780 Captured and held by British

■ British successes
▨ Colonists' successes
➤ Cornwallis' march 1781

Europeans fighting on the side of the colonists: from Poland, Kosciusko, Pulaski and von Steuben; from France, Lafayette; from Bavaria, de Kalb

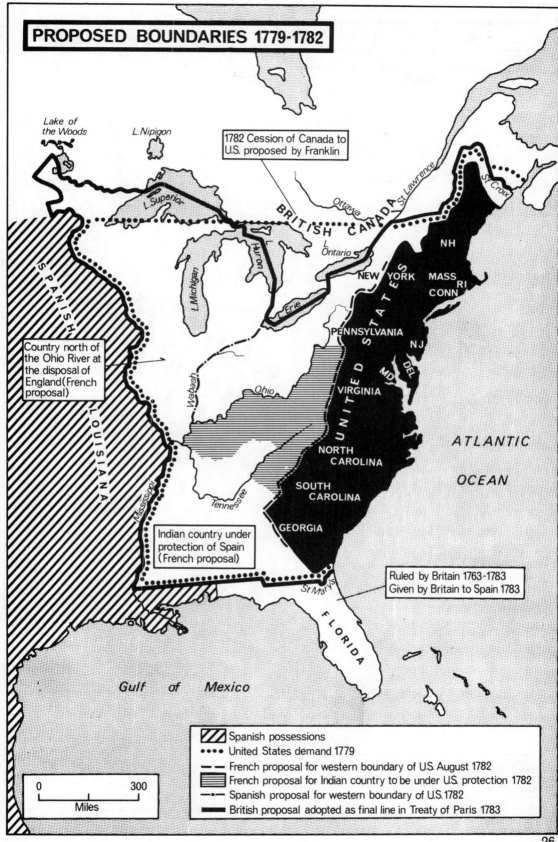

PROPOSED BOUNDARIES 1779-1782

Lake of the Woods

L. Nipigon

1782 Cession of Canada to U.S. proposed by Franklin

BRITISH CANADA

Ottawa

St Lawrence

St Croix

L. Superior

L. Huron

L. Michigan

L. Ontario

Erie

NH

NEW YORK

MASS

RI

CONN

SPANISH LOUISIANA

Country north of the Ohio River at the disposal of England (French proposal)

PENNSYLVANIA

NJ

DEL

MD

UNITED STATES

VIRGINIA

Wabash

Ohio

NORTH CAROLINA

ATLANTIC

OCEAN

Tennessee

SOUTH CAROLINA

Mississippi

Indian country under protection of Spain (French proposal)

GEORGIA

Ruled by Britain 1763-1783
Given by Britain to Spain 1783

St Mary's

FLORIDA

Gulf of Mexico

/// Spanish possessions
•••• United States demand 1779
— — — French proposal for western boundary of U.S. August 1782
≡≡≡ French proposal for Indian country to be under U.S. protection 1782
—·—·— Spanish proposal for western boundary of U.S. 1782
▬▬▬ British proposal adopted as final line in Treaty of Paris 1783

0   300

Miles

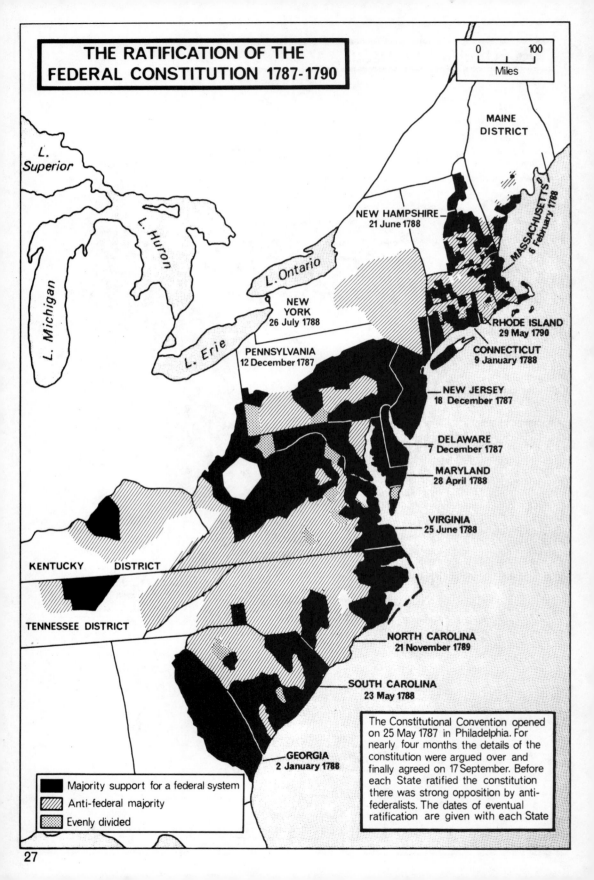

THE RATIFICATION OF THE FEDERAL CONSTITUTION 1787-1790

0   100
Miles

MAINE
DISTRICT

L. Superior

L. Huron

L. Michigan

L. Ontario

L. Erie

NEW HAMPSHIRE
21 June 1788

MASSACHUSETTS
6 February 1788

NEW YORK
26 July 1788

RHODE ISLAND
29 May 1790

CONNECTICUT
9 January 1788

PENNSYLVANIA
12 December 1787

NEW JERSEY
18 December 1787

DELAWARE
7 December 1787

MARYLAND
28 April 1788

VIRGINIA
25 June 1788

KENTUCKY   DISTRICT

TENNESSEE DISTRICT

NORTH CAROLINA
21 November 1789

SOUTH CAROLINA
23 May 1788

GEORGIA
2 January 1788

■ Majority support for a federal system

▨ Anti-federal majority

▒ Evenly divided

The Constitutional Convention opened on 25 May 1787 in Philadelphia. For nearly four months the details of the constitution were argued over and finally agreed on 17 September. Before each State ratified the constitution there was strong opposition by anti-federalists. The dates of eventual ratification are given with each State

NORTH AMERICA 1783

Legend:
- ■ The United States of America.
- British claims not finally ceded to U.S. until the Jay Treaty of 1795.
- British possessions.
- Spanish possessions.
- Disputed and unsettled frontiers.

ALASKA

Kodiak

1784 Russian settlement founded

UNEXPLORED TERRITORY

BAFFIN LAND

Northern limit of Spanish claims

HUDSON BAY

NEW SOUTH WALES

NEW BRITAIN

LABRADOR

NEWFOUNDLAND

Columbia

Snake

CANADA

ACADIA

NOVA SCOTIA

CALIFORNIA

Mississippi

THE UNITED STATES

Rio Grande

TEXAS

FLORIDA

BAHAMAS

MEXICO

CUBA

JAMAICA

BELIZE

MOSQUITO COAST

PANAMA

By the Treaty of Paris, 3 September 1783, Britain recognised the independence of the United States, withdrew all military and naval forces, agreed to fix the boundary of Canada by negotiation and returned Florida to Spain.

0   1000
Miles

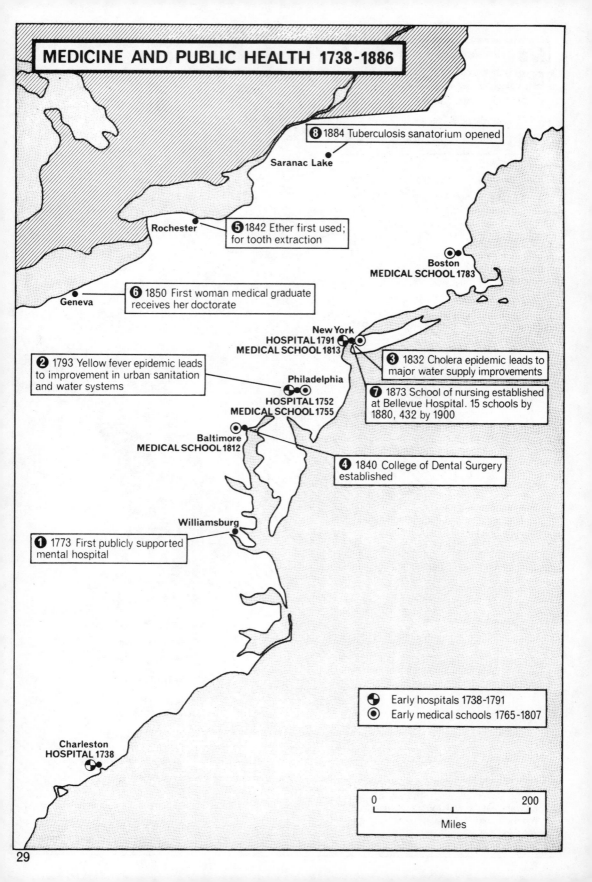

MEDICINE AND PUBLIC HEALTH 1738-1886

8 1884 Tuberculosis sanatorium opened

Saranac Lake

Rochester

5 1842 Ether first used; for tooth extraction

Boston
MEDICAL SCHOOL 1783

Geneva

6 1850 First woman medical graduate receives her doctorate

New York
HOSPITAL 1791
MEDICAL SCHOOL 1813

2 1793 Yellow fever epidemic leads to improvement in urban sanitation and water systems

3 1832 Cholera epidemic leads to major water supply improvements

Philadelphia
HOSPITAL 1752
MEDICAL SCHOOL 1755

7 1873 School of nursing established at Bellevue Hospital. 15 schools by 1880, 432 by 1900

Baltimore
MEDICAL SCHOOL 1812

4 1840 College of Dental Surgery established

Williamsburg

1 1773 First publicly supported mental hospital

Early hospitals 1738-1791
Early medical schools 1765-1807

Charleston
HOSPITAL 1738

0   200
Miles

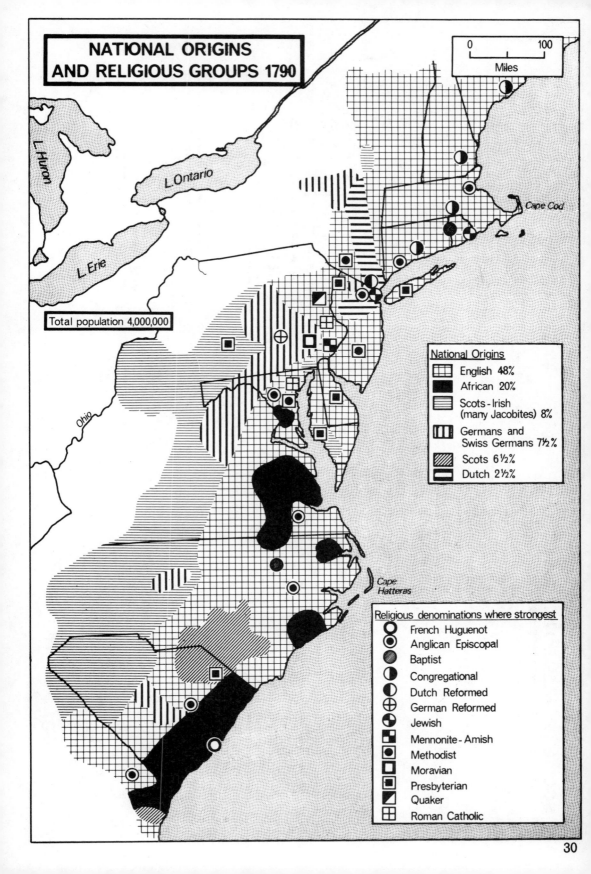

NATIONAL ORIGINS AND RELIGIOUS GROUPS 1790

0   100
Miles

Total population 4,000,000

L. Huron

L. Ontario

L. Erie

Ohio

Cape Cod

Cape Hatteras

National Origins

English 48%		
African 20%		
Scots-Irish (many Jacobites) 8%		
Germans and Swiss Germans 7½%		
Scots 6½%		
Dutch 2½%		

Religious denominations where strongest

- French Huguenot
- Anglican Episcopal
- Baptist
- Congregational
- Dutch Reformed
- German Reformed
- Jewish
- Mennonite-Amish
- Methodist
- Moravian
- Presbyterian
- Quaker
- Roman Catholic

30

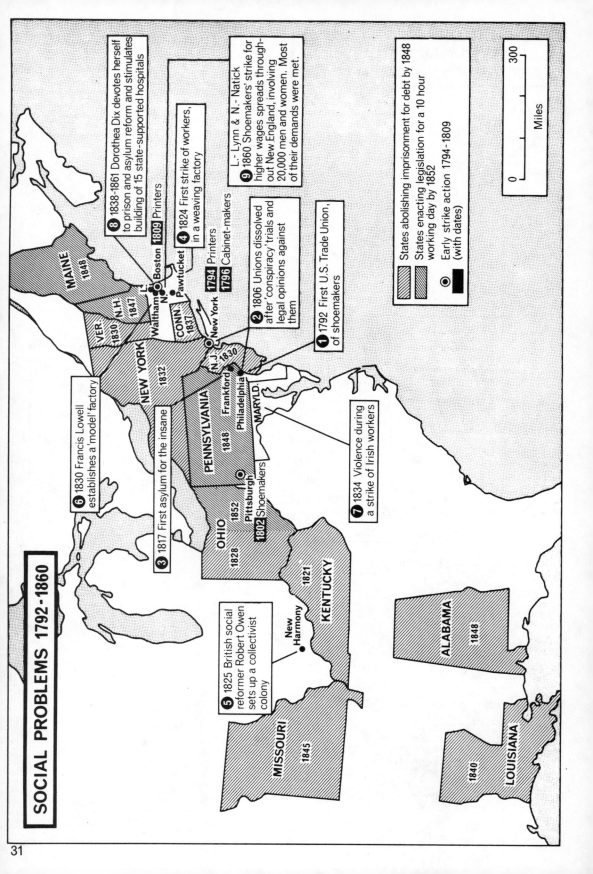

SOCIAL PROBLEMS 1792-1860

8 1838-1861 Dorothea Dix devotes herself to prison and asylum reform and stimulates building of 15 state-supported hospitals

4 1824 First strike of workers, in a weaving factory

L.- Lynn & N.- Natick
9 1860 Shoemakers' strike for higher wages spreads throughout New England, involving 20,000 men and women. Most of their demands were met.

2 1806 Unions dissolved after 'conspiracy' trials and legal opinions against them

1 1792 First U.S. Trade Union, of shoemakers

1809 Printers
Boston
Waltham
N.
Pawtucket
1794 Printers
1796 Cabinet-makers
New York
MAINE 1848
N.H. 1847
VER. 1830
CONN. 1837
NEW YORK 1832
N.J. 1830
Frankford
Philadelphia
MARYLD.
PENNSYLVANIA 1848

6 1830 Francis Lowell establishes a 'model' factory

3 1817 First asylum for the insane

7 1834 Violence during a strike of Irish workers

OHIO 1828 1852
Pittsburgh
1802 Shoemakers

5 1825 British social reformer Robert Owen sets up a collectivist colony

New Harmony

KENTUCKY 1821

MISSOURI 1845

ALABAMA 1848

LOUISIANA 1840

States abolishing imprisonment for debt by 1848

States enacting legislation for a 10 hour working day by 1852

Early strike action 1794-1809 (with dates)

0   300
Miles

31

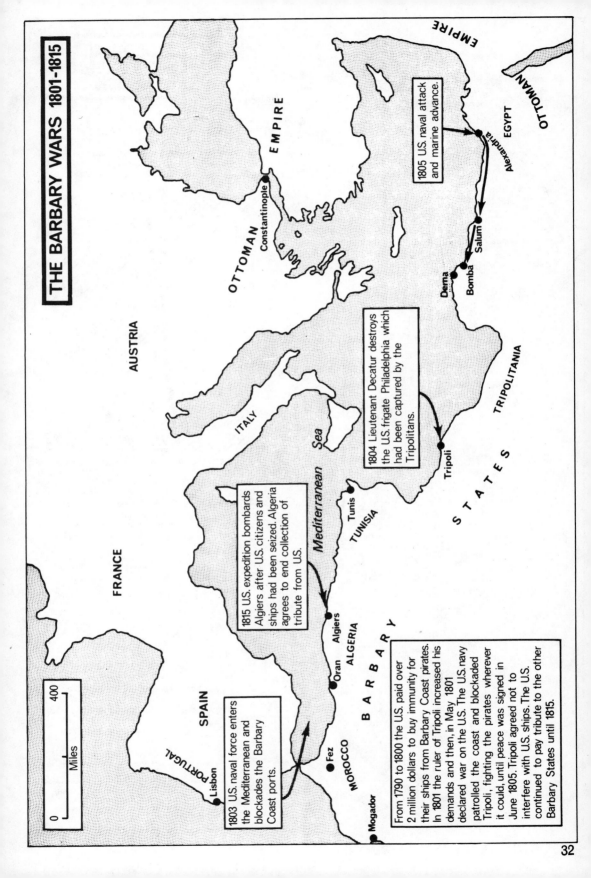

THE BARBARY WARS 1801-1815

OTTOMAN EMPIRE

OTTOMAN EMPIRE

Constantinople

AUSTRIA

ITALY

FRANCE

SPAIN

PORTUGAL

Lisbon

Mediterranean Sea

Tunis

TUNISIA

Tripoli

Alexandria

Salum

Bomba

Derna

EGYPT

TRIPOLITANIA

S T A T E S

Algiers

Oran

ALGERIA

B A R B A R Y

Fez

MOROCCO

Mogador

1815 U.S. expedition bombards Algiers after U.S. citizens and ships had been seized. Algeria agrees to end collection of tribute from U.S.

1805 U.S. naval attack and marine advance.

1804 Lieutenant Decatur destroys the U.S. frigate Philadelphia which had been captured by the Tripolitans.

1803 U.S. naval force enters the Mediterranean and blockades the Barbary Coast ports.

From 1790 to 1800 the U.S. paid over 2 million dollars to buy immunity for their ships from Barbary Coast pirates. In 1801 the ruler of Tripoli increased his demands and then, in May 1801 declared war on the U.S. The U.S. navy patrolled the coast and blockaded Tripoli, fighting the pirates wherever it could, until peace was signed in June 1805. Tripoli agreed not to interfere with U.S. ships. The U.S. continued to pay tribute to the other Barbary States until 1815.

0   400
Miles

32

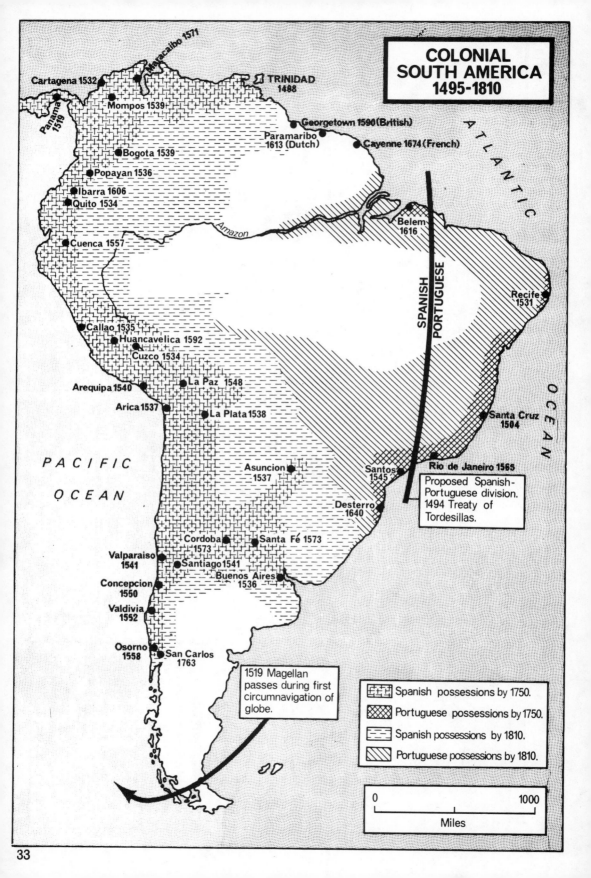

COLONIAL SOUTH AMERICA 1495-1810

Maracaibo 1571

Cartagena 1532

TRINIDAD 1488

Panama 1519

Mompos 1539

Georgetown 1590 (British)

Paramaribo 1613 (Dutch)

Cayenne 1674 (French)

Bogota 1539

Popayan 1536

Ibarra 1606

Quito 1534

Amazon

Belem 1616

Cuenca 1557

SPANISH

PORTUGUESE

ATLANTIC

Recife 1531

Callao 1535

Huancavelica 1592

Cuzco 1534

Arequipa 1540

La Paz 1548

Arica 1537

La Plata 1538

Santa Cruz 1504

OCEAN

PACIFIC OCEAN

Asuncion 1537

Santos 1545

Rio de Janeiro 1565

Desterro 1640

Proposed Spanish-Portuguese division. 1494 Treaty of Tordesillas.

Cordoba 1573

Santa Fé 1573

Valparaiso 1541

Santiago 1541

Buenos Aires 1536

Concepcion 1550

Valdivia 1552

Osorno 1558

San Carlos 1763

1519 Magellan passes during first circumnavigation of globe.

Spanish possessions by 1750.

Portuguese possessions by 1750.

Spanish possessions by 1810.

Portuguese possessions by 1810.

0   1000

Miles

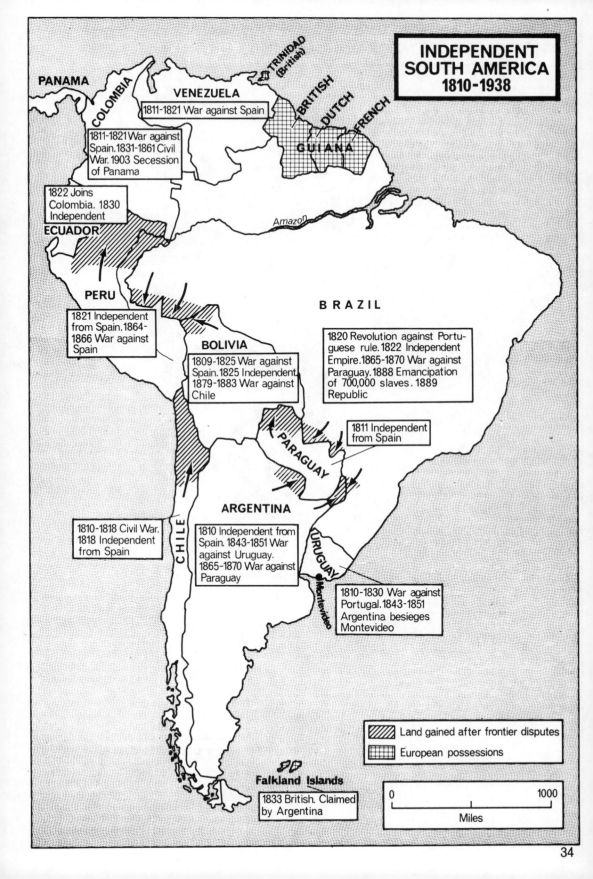

INDEPENDENT SOUTH AMERICA 1810-1938

PANAMA

COLOMBIA

VENEZUELA

1811-1821 War against Spain

1811-1821 War against Spain. 1831-1861 Civil War. 1903 Secession of Panama

TRINIDAD (British)

BRITISH DUTCH FRENCH GUIANA

1822 Joins Colombia. 1830 Independent

ECUADOR

Amazon

PERU

1821 Independent from Spain. 1864-1866 War against Spain

BRAZIL

BOLIVIA

1809-1825 War against Spain. 1825 Independent. 1879-1883 War against Chile

1820 Revolution against Portuguese rule. 1822 Independent Empire. 1865-1870 War against Paraguay. 1888 Emancipation of 700,000 slaves. 1889 Republic

PARAGUAY

1811 Independent from Spain

1810-1818 Civil War. 1818 Independent from Spain

CHILE

ARGENTINA

1810 Independent from Spain. 1843-1851 War against Uruguay. 1865-1870 War against Paraguay

URUGUAY

Montevideo

1810-1830 War against Portugal. 1843-1851 Argentina besieges Montevideo

Land gained after frontier disputes

European possessions

Falkland Islands

1833 British. Claimed by Argentina

0   1000
Miles

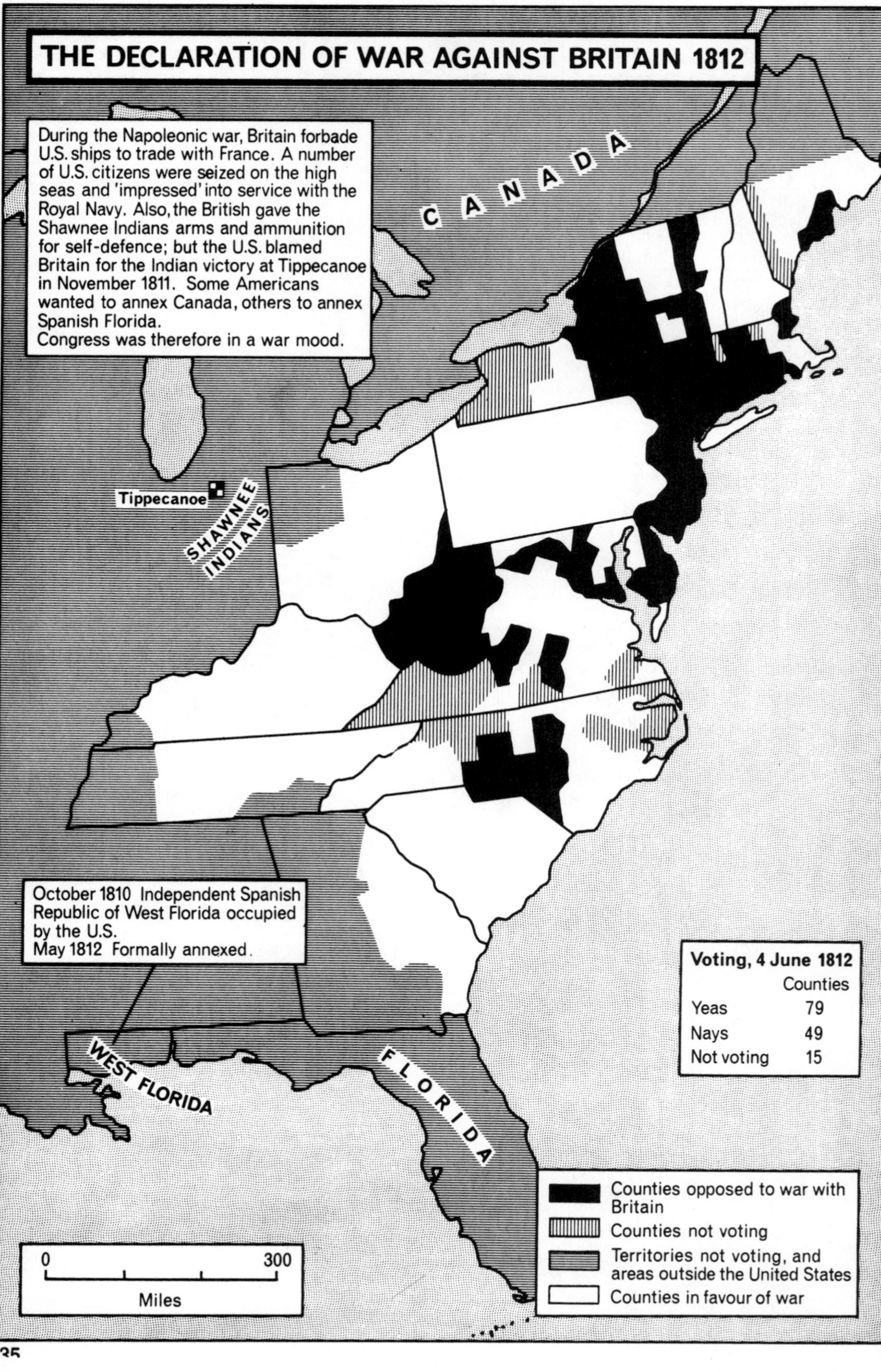

THE DECLARATION OF WAR AGAINST BRITAIN 1812

During the Napoleonic war, Britain forbade U.S. ships to trade with France. A number of U.S. citizens were seized on the high seas and 'impressed' into service with the Royal Navy. Also, the British gave the Shawnee Indians arms and ammunition for self-defence; but the U.S. blamed Britain for the Indian victory at Tippecanoe in November 1811. Some Americans wanted to annex Canada, others to annex Spanish Florida.
Congress was therefore in a war mood.

CANADA

Tippecanoe

SHAWNEE INDIANS

October 1810 Independent Spanish Republic of West Florida occupied by the U.S.
May 1812 Formally annexed.

WEST FLORIDA

FLORIDA

Voting, 4 June 1812

	Counties
Yeas	79
Nays	49
Not voting	15

■ Counties opposed to war with Britain

▥ Counties not voting

▨ Territories not voting, and areas outside the United States

☐ Counties in favour of war

0   300

Miles

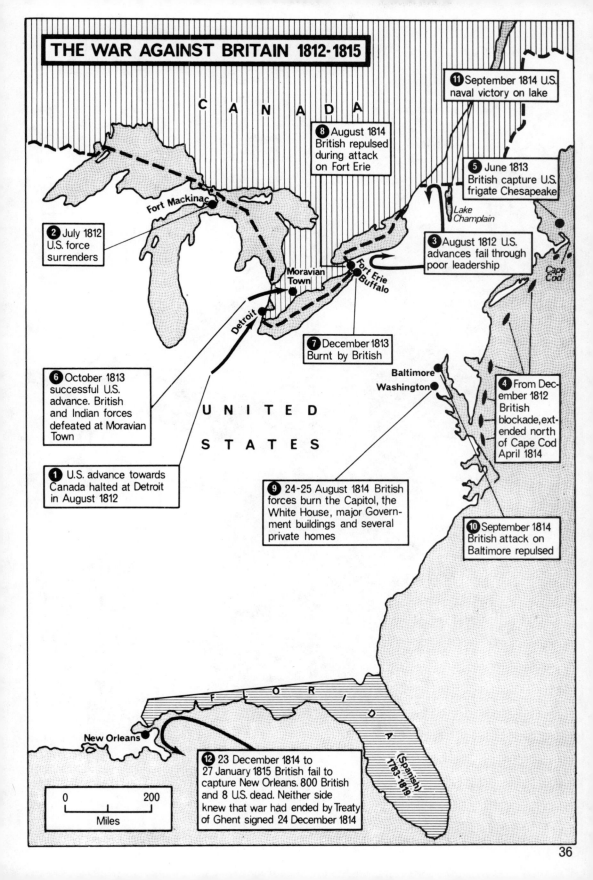

THE WAR AGAINST BRITAIN 1812-1815

C A N A D A

11 September 1814 U.S. naval victory on lake

8 August 1814 British repulsed during attack on Fort Erie

5 June 1813 British capture U.S. frigate Chesapeake

Lake Champlain

Fort Mackinac

2 July 1812 U.S. force surrenders

Cape Cod

3 August 1812 U.S. advances fail through poor leadership

Moravian Town

Fort Erie
Buffalo

Detroit

7 December 1813 Burnt by British

6 October 1813 successful U.S. advance. British and Indian forces defeated at Moravian Town

Baltimore
Washington

4 From December 1812 British blockade, extended north of Cape Cod April 1814

U N I T E D
S T A T E S

1 U.S. advance towards Canada halted at Detroit in August 1812

9 24-25 August 1814 British forces burn the Capitol, the White House, major Government buildings and several private homes

10 September 1814 British attack on Baltimore repulsed

F L O R I D A

(Spanish) 1783-1819

New Orleans

12 23 December 1814 to 27 January 1815 British fail to capture New Orleans. 800 British and 8 U.S. dead. Neither side knew that war had ended by Treaty of Ghent signed 24 December 1814

0   200
Miles

36

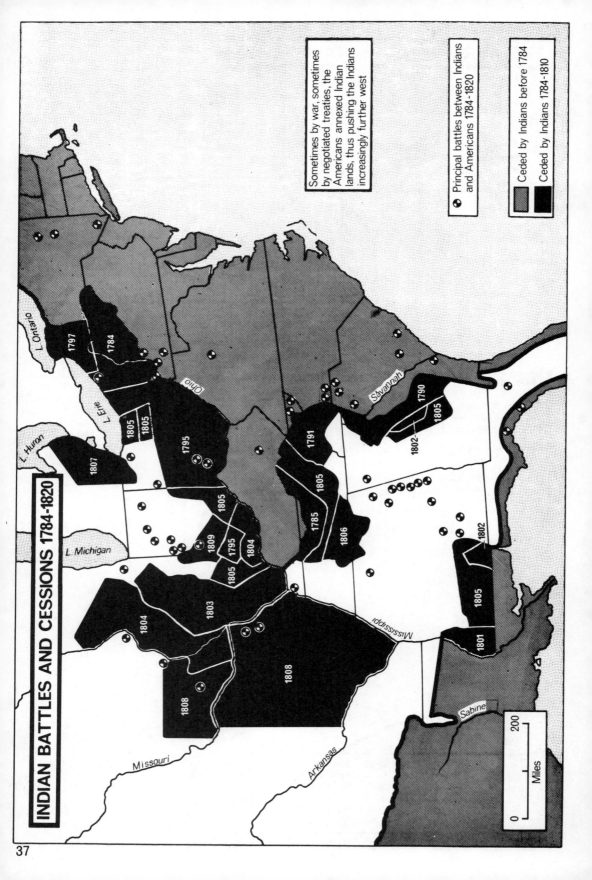

INDIAN BATTLES AND CESSIONS 1784-1820

Sometimes by war, sometimes by negotiated treaties, the Americans annexed Indian lands, thus pushing the Indians increasingly further west

- Principal battles between Indians and Americans 1784-1820

Ceded by Indians before 1784

Ceded by Indians 1784-1810

L. Ontario

L. Erie

L. Huron

L. Michigan

Ohio

Savannah

Mississippi

Missouri

Arkansas

Sabine

1797

1784

1805

1805

1807

1795

1805

1809

1795

1805

1804

1803

1804

1808

1808

1791

1805

1785

1806

1790

1805

1802

1802

1805

1801

200

0

Miles

37

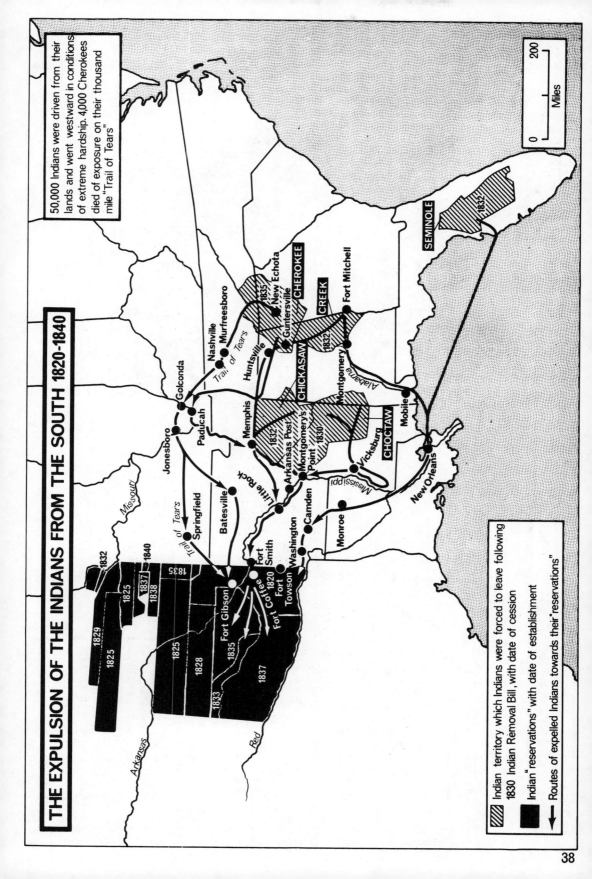

THE EXPULSION OF THE INDIANS FROM THE SOUTH 1820-1840

50,000 Indians were driven from their lands and went westward in conditions of extreme hardship. 4,000 Cherokees died of exposure on their thousand mile "Trail of Tears"

0   200
Miles

Indian territory which Indians were forced to leave following 1830 Indian Removal Bill, with date of cession

Indian "reservations" with date of establishment

Routes of expelled Indians towards their "reservations"

SEMINOLE 1832

CHEROKEE

CREEK

CHICKASAW

CHOCTAW

1835 New Echota
Guntersville
Fort Mitchell
1832
1830
Montgomery's Point
1832
Arkansas Post

Nashville
Murfreesboro
Golconda
Paducah
Jonesboro
Memphis
Huntsville
Montgomery
Mobile
New Orleans
Vicksburg
Monroe
Camden
Washington
Fort Towson
Fort Coffee 1820
Fort Smith
Fort Gibson
Little Rock
Batesville
Springfield

Trail of Tears

Missouri
Arkansas
Red
Mississippi
Alabama

1832
1829
1825
1825
1837
1840
1838
1835
1828
1833
1837

38

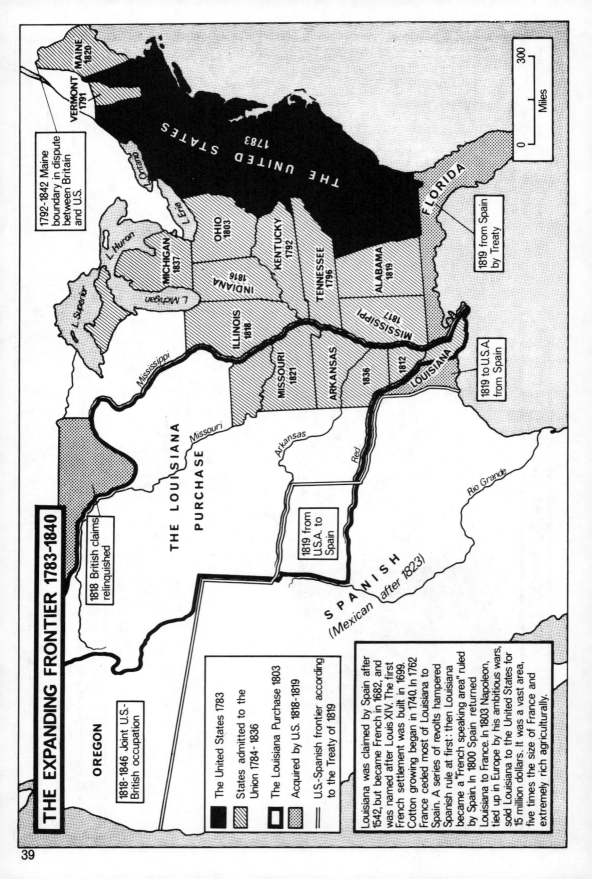

THE EXPANDING FRONTIER 1783-1840

THE UNITED STATES 1783

1792-1842 Maine boundary in dispute between Britain and U.S.

MAINE 1820

VERMONT 1791

L. Ontario

L. Erie

L. Huron

L. Superior

MICHIGAN 1837

L. Michigan

OHIO 1803

INDIANA 1816

ILLINOIS 1818

KENTUCKY 1792

TENNESSEE 1796

ALABAMA 1819

MISSISSIPPI 1817

FLORIDA

1819 from Spain by Treaty

MISSOURI 1821

ARKANSAS

1836

1812

LOUISIANA

1819 to U.S.A. from Spain

Mississippi

THE LOUISIANA PURCHASE

Missouri

Arkansas

Red

1819 from U.S.A. to Spain

Rio Grande

S P A N I S H
(Mexican after 1823)

OREGON

1818-1846 Joint U.S.-British occupation

1818 British claims relinquished

0   300
Miles

Louisiana was claimed by Spain after 1542, but became French in 1682, and was named after Louis XIV. The first French settlement was built in 1699. Cotton growing began in 1740. In 1762 France ceded most of Louisiana to Spain. A series of revolts hampered Spanish rule at first: then Louisiana became a "French speaking area" ruled by Spain. In 1800 Spain returned Louisiana to France. In 1803 Napoleon, tied up in Europe by his ambitious wars, sold Louisiana to the United States for 15 million dollars. It was a vast area, five times the size of France and extremely rich agriculturally.

The United States 1783

States admitted to the Union 1784 - 1836

The Louisiana Purchase 1803

Acquired by U.S. 1818-1819

U.S.-Spanish frontier according to the Treaty of 1819

39

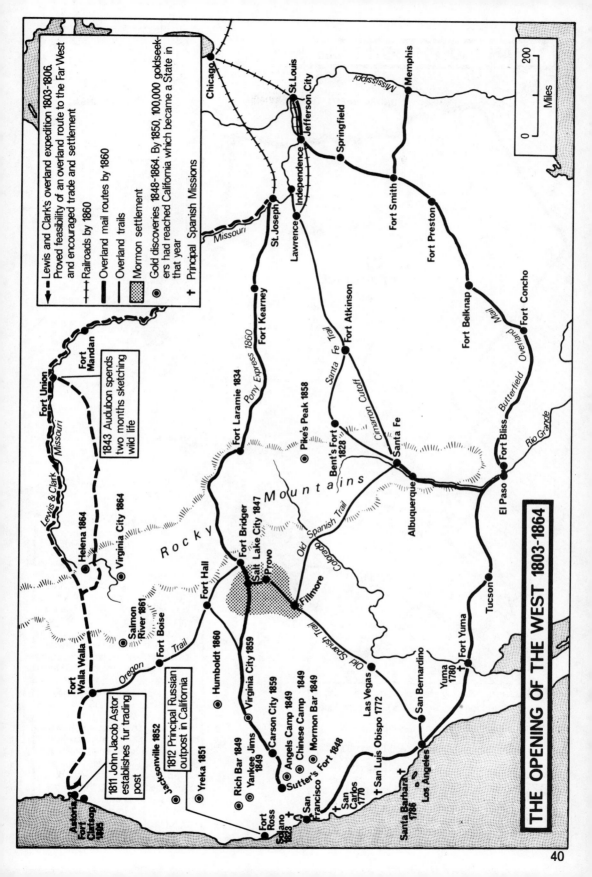

THE OPENING OF THE WEST 1803-1864

Legend:
- Lewis and Clark's overland expedition 1803-1806. Proved feasibility of an overland route to the Far West and encouraged trade and settlement
- Railroads by 1860
- Overland mail routes by 1860
- Overland trails
- Mormon settlement
- Gold discoveries 1848-1864. By 1850, 100,000 goldseekers had reached California which became a State in that year
- + Principal Spanish Missions

1843 Audubon spends two months sketching wild life

1811 John Jacob Astor establishes fur trading post

1812 Principal Russian outpost in California

Labels on map:

Chicago
St. Louis
Jefferson City
Memphis
Springfield
Independence
Lawrence
St. Joseph
Fort Smith
Fort Preston
Fort Concho
Fort Belknap
Fort Bliss
El Paso
Fort Kearney
Fort Atkinson
Santa Fe
Albuquerque
Tucson
Fort Yuma
Fort Laramie 1834
Pony Express 1860
Pike's Peak 1858
Bent's Fort 1828
Santa Fe Trail
Cimarron Cutoff
Old Spanish Trail
Butterfield Overland Mail
Rio Grande
Colorado
Mississippi
Missouri
Fort Union
Fort Mandan
Lewis & Clark
Helena 1864
Virginia City 1864
Salmon River 1861
Fort Boise
Fort Walla Walla
Astoria Fort Clatsop 1805
Jacksonville 1852
Yreka 1851
Rich Bar 1849
Yankee Jims 1849
Humboldt 1860
Virginia City 1859
Carson City 1859
Angels Camp 1849
Chinese Camp 1849
Mormon Bar 1849
Sutter's Fort 1848
San Francisco
Fort Ross
Solano 1823
San Carlos 1770
San Luis Obispo 1772
Santa Barbara 1786
Los Angeles
San Bernardino
Las Vegas
Yuma 1780
Fort Hall
Fort Bridger
Salt Lake City 1847
Provo
Fillmore
Oregon Trail
Rocky Mountains

Miles 0 — 200

40

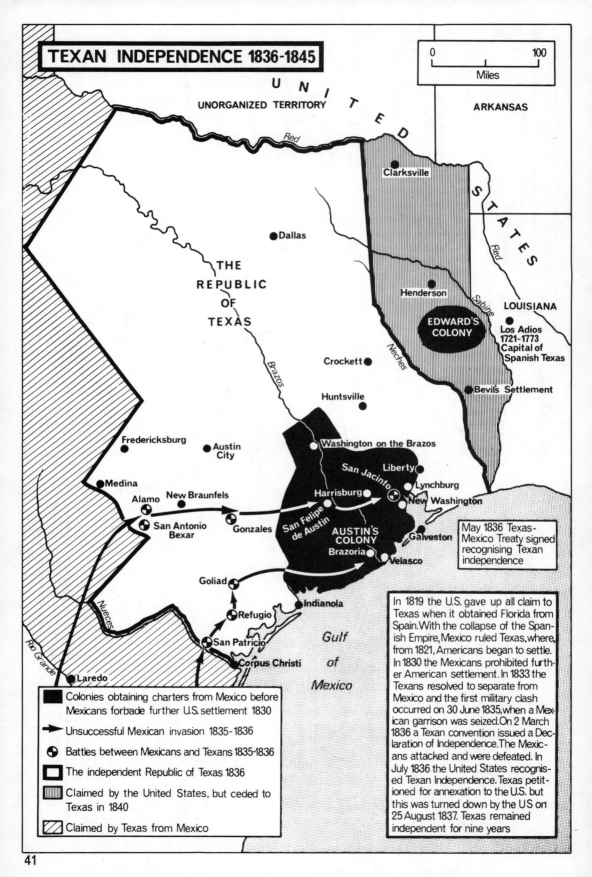

TEXAN INDEPENDENCE 1836-1845

0 100
Miles

U N I T E D

UNORGANIZED TERRITORY

ARKANSAS

S T A T E S

Red

Clarksville

Dallas

THE
REPUBLIC
OF
TEXAS

Henderson

LOUISIANA

EDWARD'S
COLONY

Los Adios
1721-1773
Capital of
Spanish Texas

Red

Sabine

Neches

Brazos

Crockett

Huntsville

Bevils Settlement

Fredericksburg

Austin
City

Washington on the Brazos

Liberty

San Jacinto

Medina

Lynchburg

Alamo

New Braunfels

Harrisburg

New Washington

San Antonio
Bexar

Gonzales

San Felipe
de Austin

AUSTIN'S
COLONY

Galveston

May 1836 Texas-
Mexico Treaty signed
recognising Texan
independence

Brazoria

Velasco

Goliad

Indianola

Refugio

Gulf

San Patricio

Nueces

Corpus Christi

of

Rio Grande

Laredo

Mexico

In 1819 the U.S. gave up all claim to
Texas when it obtained Florida from
Spain. With the collapse of the Spanish Empire, Mexico ruled Texas, where,
from 1821, Americans began to settle.
In 1830 the Mexicans prohibited further American settlement. In 1833 the
Texans resolved to separate from
Mexico and the first military clash
occurred on 30 June 1835, when a Mexican garrison was seized. On 2 March
1836 a Texan convention issued a Declaration of Independence. The Mexicans attacked and were defeated. In
July 1836 the United States recognised Texan Independence. Texas petit-
ioned for annexation to the U.S. but
this was turned down by the US on
25 August 1837. Texas remained
independent for nine years

■ Colonies obtaining charters from Mexico before
Mexicans forbade further U.S. settlement 1830

→ Unsuccessful Mexican invasion 1835-1836

✛ Battles between Mexicans and Texans 1835-1836

□ The independent Republic of Texas 1836

▥ Claimed by the United States, but ceded to
Texas in 1840

▨ Claimed by Texas from Mexico

41

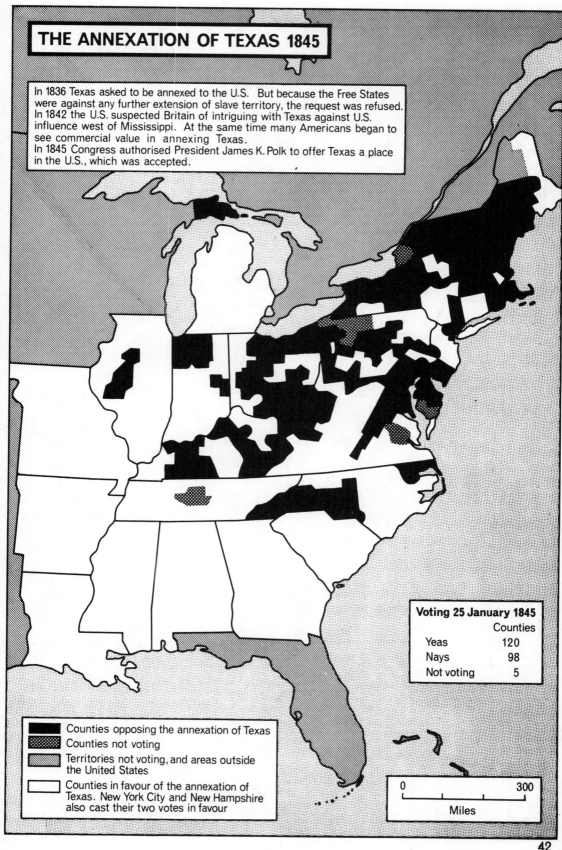

THE ANNEXATION OF TEXAS 1845

In 1836 Texas asked to be annexed to the U.S. But because the Free States were against any further extension of slave territory, the request was refused. In 1842 the U.S. suspected Britain of intriguing with Texas against U.S. influence west of Mississippi. At the same time many Americans began to see commercial value in annexing Texas.
In 1845 Congress authorised President James K. Polk to offer Texas a place in the U.S., which was accepted.

Voting 25 January 1845

	Counties
Yeas	120
Nays	98
Not voting	5

Counties opposing the annexation of Texas

Counties not voting

Territories not voting, and areas outside the United States

Counties in favour of the annexation of Texas. New York City and New Hampshire also cast their two votes in favour

0   300

Miles

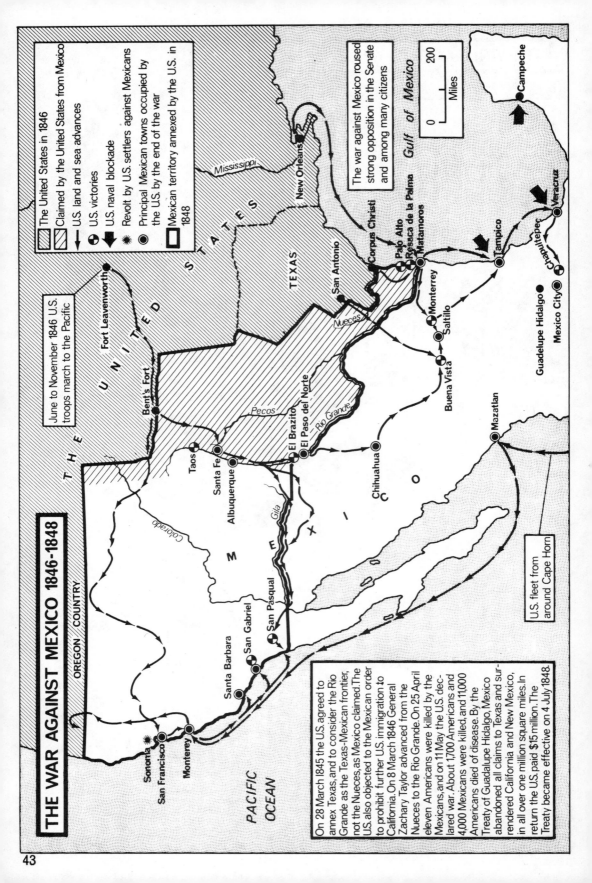

THE WAR AGAINST MEXICO 1846-1848

OREGON COUNTRY

THE UNITED STATES

TEXAS

PACIFIC OCEAN

Gulf of Mexico

June to November 1846 U.S.
troops march to the Pacific

The war against Mexico roused
strong opposition in the Senate
and among many citizens

The United States in 1846

Claimed by the United States from Mexico

→ U.S. land and sea advances

U.S. victories

U.S. naval blockade

Revolt by U.S. settlers against Mexicans

Principal Mexican towns occupied by
the U.S. by the end of the war

Mexican territory annexed by the U.S. in
1848

0   200
Miles

Mississippi

New Orleans

Fort Leavenworth

Bent's Fort

Taos
Santa Fe
Albuquerque

Pecos
El Brazito
El Paso del Norte
Rio Grande

Nueces

San Antonio

Corpus Christi
Palo Alto
Resaca de la Palma
Matamoros

Monterrey
Saltillo
Buena Vista

Chihuahua

MEXICO

Colorado
Gila

San Pasqual

San Gabriel
Santa Barbara

Monterey

San Francisco
Sonoma

Mazatlan

Tampico
Chapultepec
Veracruz

Guadalupe Hidalgo
Mexico City

Campeche

U.S. fleet from
around Cape Horn

On 28 March 1845 the U.S. agreed to
annex Texas, and to consider the Rio
Grande as the Texas-Mexican frontier,
not the Nueces, as Mexico claimed. The
U.S. also objected to the Mexican order
to prohibit further U.S. immigration to
California. On 8 March 1846 General
Zachary Taylor advanced from the
Nueces to the Rio Grande. On 25 April
eleven Americans were killed by the
Mexicans, and on 11 May the U.S. declared war. About 1,700 Americans and
4,000 Mexicans were killed, and 11,000
Americans died of disease. By the
Treaty of Guadalupe Hidalgo, Mexico
abandoned all claims to Texas and surrendered California and New Mexico,
in all over one million square miles. In
return the U.S. paid $15 million. The
Treaty became effective on 4 July 1848.

43

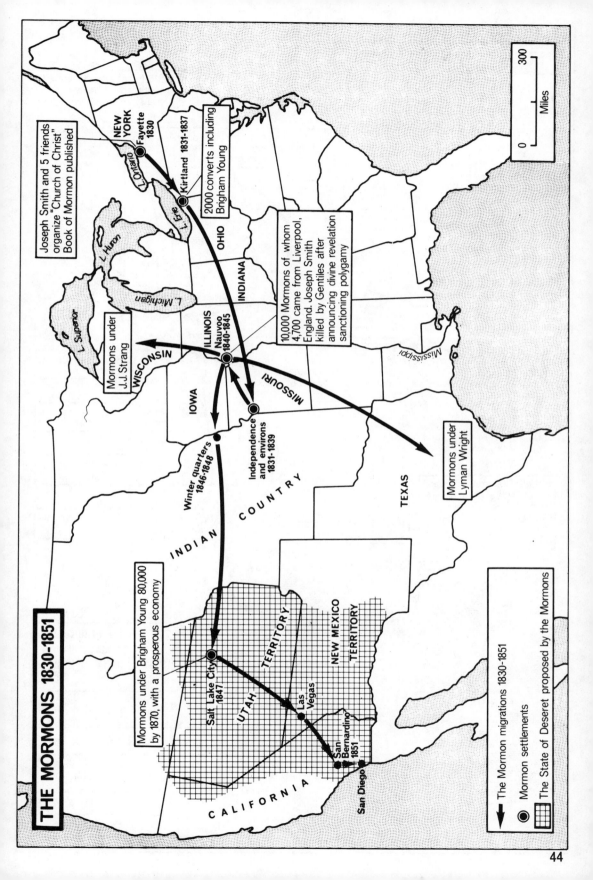

THE MORMONS 1830-1851

Joseph Smith and 5 friends organize "Church of Christ" Book of Mormon published

NEW YORK Fayette 1830

L. Ontario

L. Erie

Kirtland 1831-1837

2000 converts including Brigham Young

OHIO

INDIANA

L. Huron

L. Michigan

L. Superior

10,000 Mormons of whom 4,700 came from Liverpool, England. Joseph Smith killed by Gentiles after announcing divine revelation sanctioning polygamy

Mormons under J.J. Strang

WISCONSIN

ILLINOIS Nauvoo 1840-1845

IOWA

MISSOURI

Mississippi

Winter quarters 1846-1848

Independence and environs 1831-1839

INDIAN COUNTRY

Mormons under Lyman Wright

TEXAS

Mormons under Brigham Young 80,000 by 1870, with a prosperous economy

Salt Lake City 1847

UTAH TERRITORY

NEW MEXICO TERRITORY

Las Vegas

San Bernardino 1851

San Diego

CALIFORNIA

0 — 300 Miles

The Mormon migrations 1830-1851

● Mormon settlements

The State of Deseret proposed by the Mormons

44

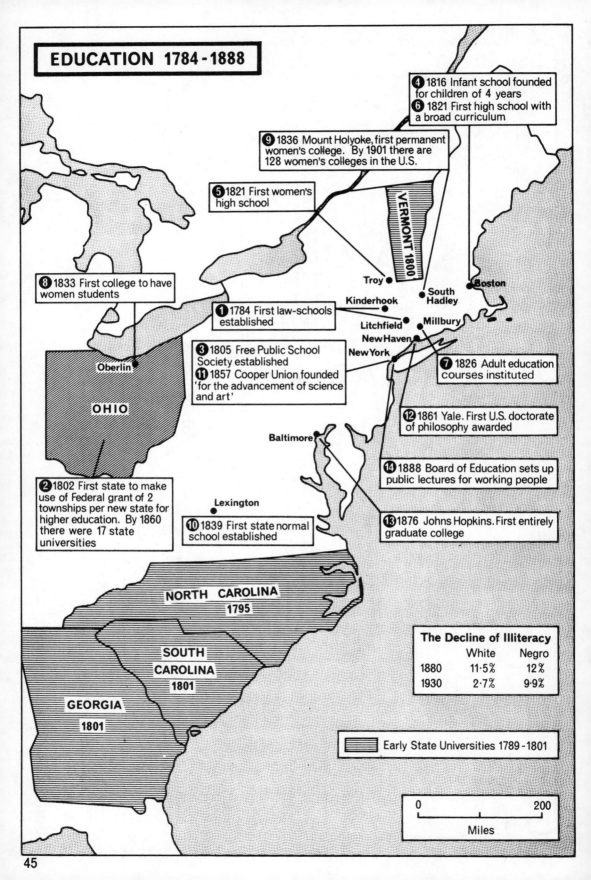

EDUCATION 1784 - 1888

4 1816 Infant school founded for children of 4 years

6 1821 First high school with a broad curriculum

9 1836 Mount Holyoke, first permanent women's college. By 1901 there are 128 women's colleges in the U.S.

5 1821 First women's high school

VERMONT 1800

8 1833 First college to have women students

1 1784 First law-schools established

Troy

Kinderhook

South Hadley

Boston

Litchfield

Millbury

New Haven

New York

3 1805 Free Public School Society established

11 1857 Cooper Union founded 'for the advancement of science and art'

Oberlin

OHIO

7 1826 Adult education courses instituted

12 1861 Yale. First U.S. doctorate of philosophy awarded

Baltimore

14 1888 Board of Education sets up public lectures for working people

2 1802 First state to make use of Federal grant of 2 townships per new state for higher education. By 1860 there were 17 state universities

Lexington

10 1839 First state normal school established

13 1876 Johns Hopkins. First entirely graduate college

NORTH CAROLINA 1795

SOUTH CAROLINA 1801

GEORGIA 1801

The Decline of Illiteracy		
	White	Negro
1880	11·5%	12%
1930	2·7%	9·9%

Early State Universities 1789 -1801

0   200

Miles

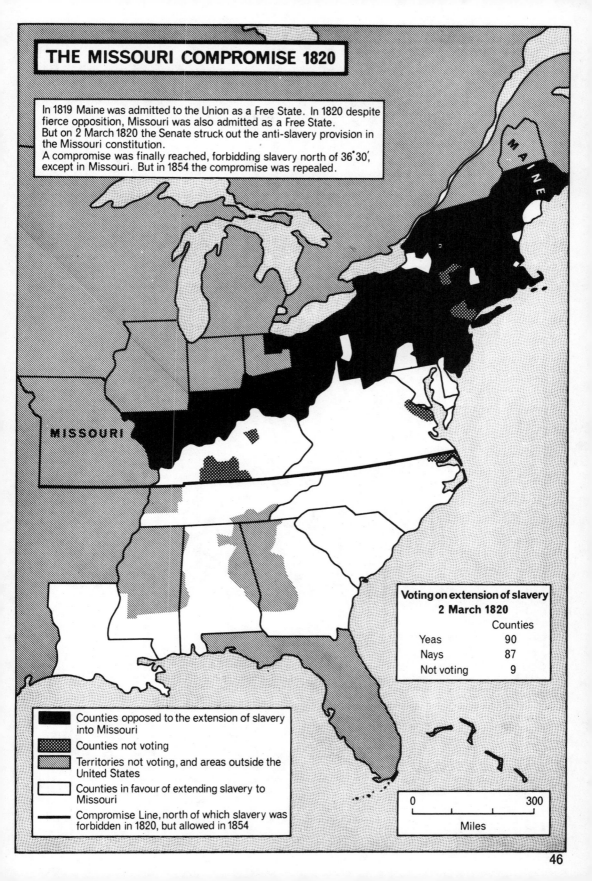

THE MISSOURI COMPROMISE 1820

In 1819 Maine was admitted to the Union as a Free State. In 1820 despite fierce opposition, Missouri was also admitted as a Free State.
But on 2 March 1820 the Senate struck out the anti-slavery provision in the Missouri constitution.
A compromise was finally reached, forbidding slavery north of 36°30', except in Missouri. But in 1854 the compromise was repealed.

MAINE

MISSOURI

**Voting on extension of slavery
2 March 1820**

	Counties
Yeas	90
Nays	87
Not voting	9

Counties opposed to the extension of slavery into Missouri

Counties not voting

Territories not voting, and areas outside the United States

Counties in favour of extending slavery to Missouri

Compromise Line, north of which slavery was forbidden in 1820, but allowed in 1854

0   300

Miles

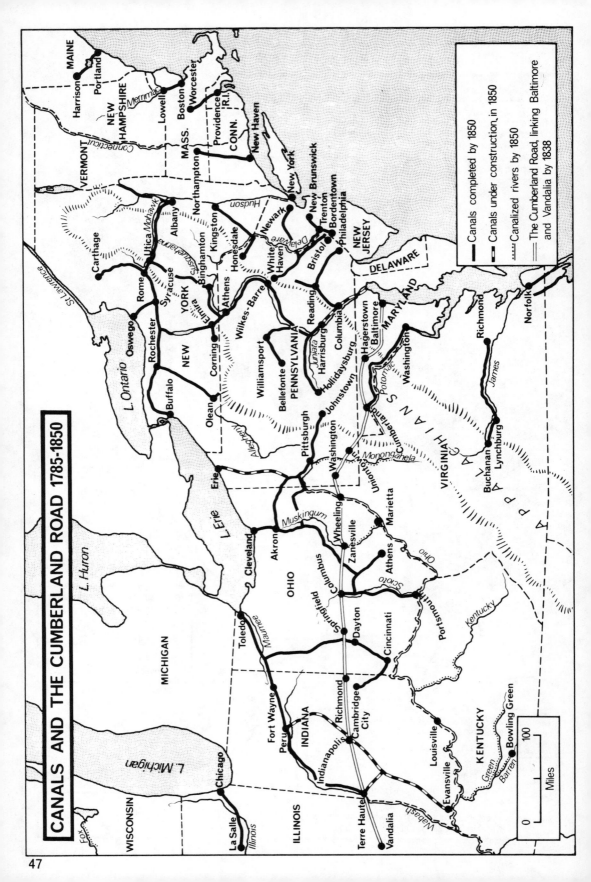

CANALS AND THE CUMBERLAND ROAD 1785-1850

Legend:
— Canals completed by 1850
▭ Canals under construction in 1850
- - - - Canalized rivers by 1850
═══ The Cumberland Road, linking Baltimore and Vandalia by 1838

47

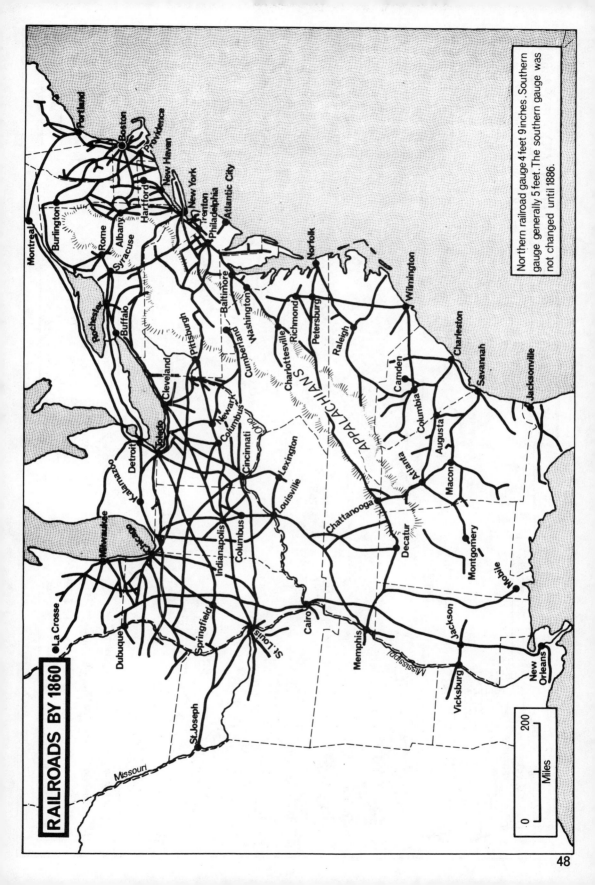

RAILROADS BY 1860

Northern railroad gauge 4 feet 9 inches. Southern gauge generally 5 feet. The southern gauge was not changed until 1886.

200

0

Miles

APPALACHIANS

Portland
Boston
Providence
New Haven
Hartford
New York
Trenton
Philadelphia
Atlantic City
Montreal
Burlington
Rome
Albany
Syracuse
Rochester
Buffalo
Pittsburgh
Baltimore
Cumberland
Washington
Norfolk
Richmond
Petersburg
Charlottesville
Raleigh
Wilmington
Charleston
Savannah
Jacksonville
Camden
Columbia
Augusta
Macon
Atlanta
Cleveland
Toledo
Detroit
Kalamazoo
Milwaukee
Chicago
Newark
Columbus
Cincinnati
Lexington
Louisville
Chattanooga
Decatur
Montgomery
Mobile
La Crosse
Dubuque
Springfield
Indianapolis
Columbus
St. Louis
Cairo
Memphis
Jackson
Vicksburg
New Orleans
St. Joseph
Missouri
Mississippi
Ohio

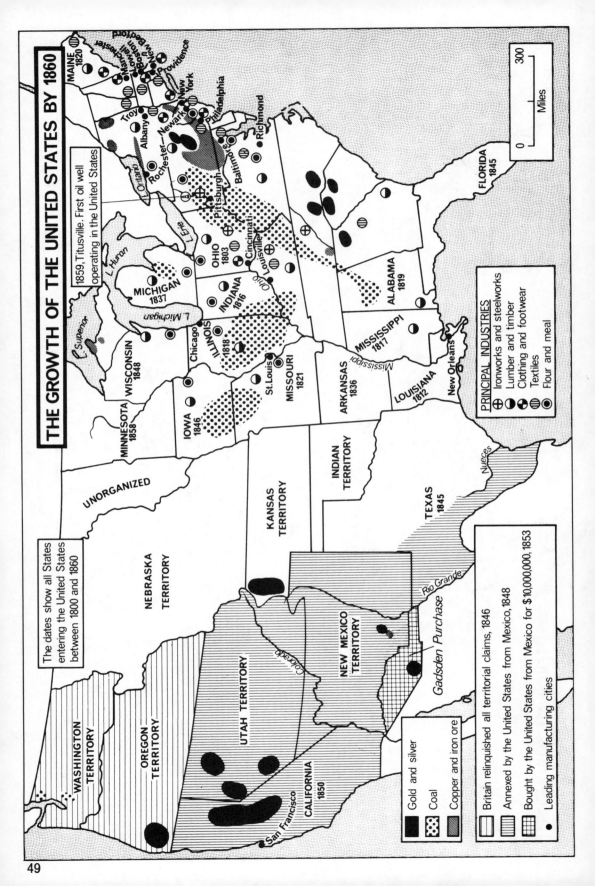

THE GROWTH OF THE UNITED STATES BY 1860

1859, Titusville. First oil well operating in the United States

The dates show all States entering the United States between 1800 and 1860

MAINE 1820

FLORIDA 1845

Troy
Albany
Rochester
Newark
Philadelphia
Pittsburgh
Baltimore
Richmond
OHIO 1803
Cincinnati
Louisville
Chicago
St. Louis
New Orleans

L. Superior
L. Huron
L. Michigan
L. Erie
L. Ontario

MICHIGAN 1837
WISCONSIN 1848
MINNESOTA 1858
IOWA 1846
ILLINOIS 1818
INDIANA 1816
MISSOURI 1821
ARKANSAS 1836
MISSISSIPPI 1817
ALABAMA 1819
LOUISIANA 1812

Mississippi
Ohio

UNORGANIZED
NEBRASKA TERRITORY
KANSAS TERRITORY
INDIAN TERRITORY
TEXAS 1845

Nueces
Rio Grande
Colorado
Gadsden Purchase

WASHINGTON TERRITORY
OREGON TERRITORY
UTAH TERRITORY
NEW MEXICO TERRITORY
CALIFORNIA 1850
San Francisco

PRINCIPAL INDUSTRIES
⊕ Ironworks and steelworks
◑ Lumber and timber
◕ Clothing and footwear
⊖ Textiles
◉ Flour and meal

Gold and silver
Coal
Copper and iron ore

Britain relinquished all territorial claims, 1846
Annexed by the United States from Mexico, 1848
Bought by the United States from Mexico for $10,000,000, 1853
• Leading manufacturing cities

Miles
0   300

49

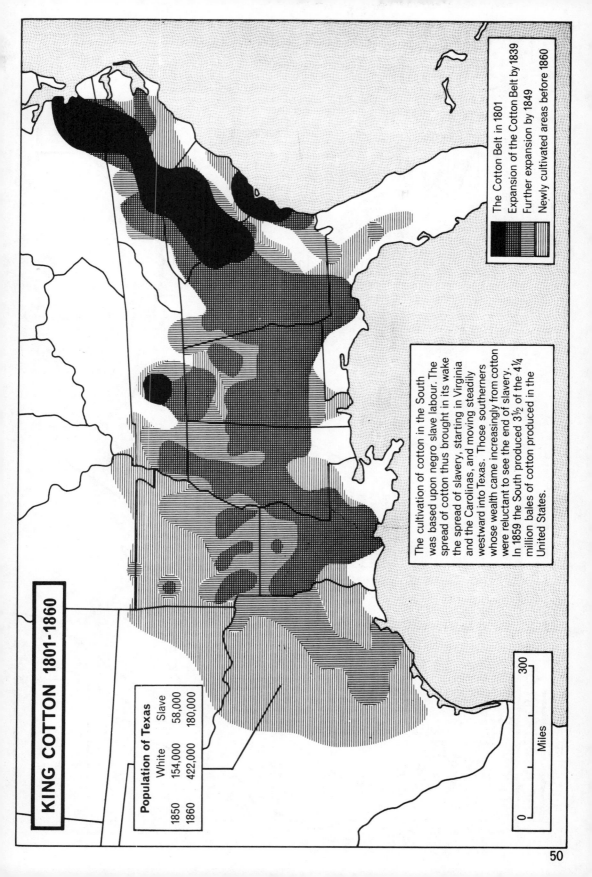

KING COTTON 1801-1860

Population of Texas

	White	Slave
1850	154,000	58,000
1860	422,000	180,000

The Cotton Belt in 1801

Expansion of the Cotton Belt by 1839

Further expansion by 1849

Newly cultivated areas before 1860

The cultivation of cotton in the South was based upon negro slave labour. The spread of cotton thus brought in its wake the spread of slavery, starting in Virginia and the Carolinas, and moving steadily westward into Texas. Those southerners whose wealth came increasingly from cotton were reluctant to see the end of slavery. In 1859 the South produced 3½ of the 4¼ million bales of cotton produced in the United States.

0   300

Miles

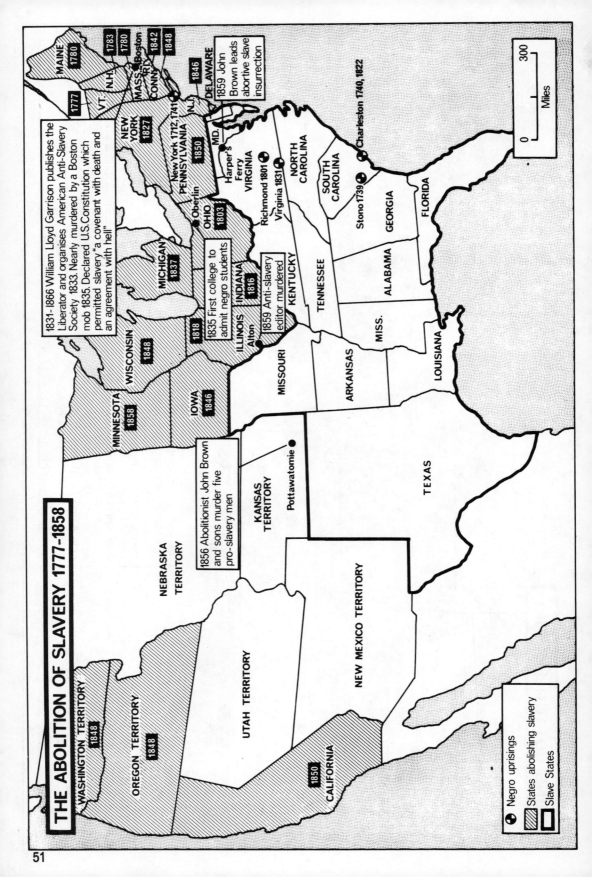

THE ABOLITION OF SLAVERY 1777-1858

MAINE 1780

N.H. 1783 1780

MASS. Boston 1773 1842

CONN. 1848

VT. 1777

DELAWARE 1846

1859 John Brown leads abortive slave insurrection

NEW YORK 1827

New York 1712, 1741 PENNSYLVANIA 1780

N.J.

MD.

Harper's Ferry VIRGINIA

Richmond 1801

Virginia 1831

NORTH CAROLINA

SOUTH CAROLINA

Charleston 1740, 1822

Stono 1739

1831-1866 William Lloyd Garrison publishes the Liberator and organises American Anti-Slavery Society 1833. Nearly murdered by a Boston mob 1835. Declared U.S.Constitution which permitted slavery "a covenant with death and an agreement with hell"

Oberlin OHIO 1803

MICHIGAN 1837

WISCONSIN 1848

1835 First college to admit negro students

INDIANA 1816

ILLINOIS 1818 Alton

1859 Anti-slavery editor murdered

KENTUCKY

TENNESSEE

MISS.

ALABAMA

GEORGIA

FLORIDA

MINNESOTA 1858

IOWA 1846

MISSOURI

ARKANSAS

LOUISIANA

1856 Abolitionist John Brown and sons murder five pro-slavery men

KANSAS TERRITORY

Pottawatomie

NEBRASKA TERRITORY

TEXAS

WASHINGTON TERRITORY 1848

OREGON TERRITORY 1848

UTAH TERRITORY

NEW MEXICO TERRITORY

CALIFORNIA 1850

300

Miles

0

⊕ Negro uprisings

▨ States abolishing slavery

☐ Slave States

51

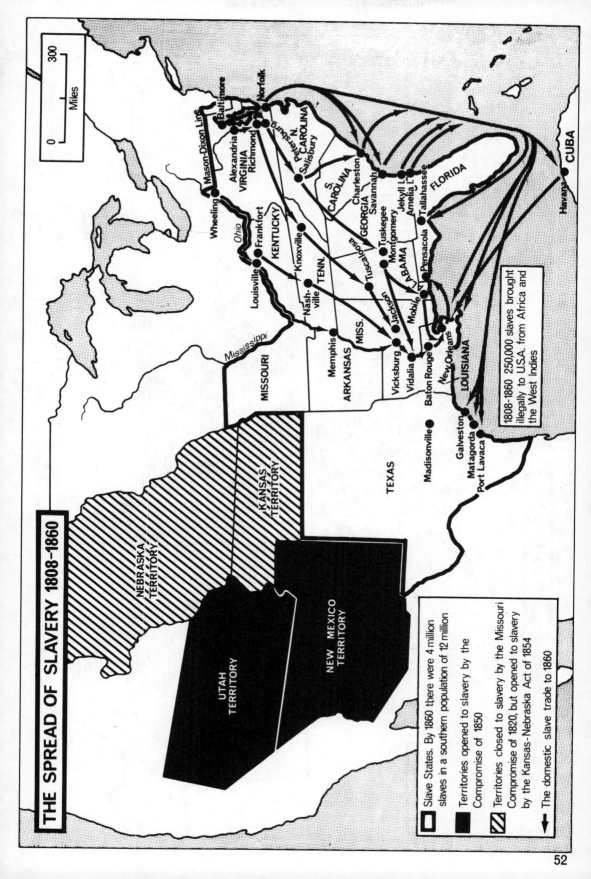

THE SPREAD OF SLAVERY 1808-1860

Mason-Dixon Line

Baltimore
Alexandria
Richmond
VIRGINIA
Wheeling
Ohio
Petersburg
Peter N.
Salisbury
S. CAROLINA
N. CAROLINA
Charleston
Savannah
GEORGIA
Jekyll I.
Amelia I.
FLORIDA
Tallahassee
Pensacola
ALABAMA
Montgomery
Tuskegee
Tuscaloosa
Mobile
Jackson
MISS.
Vicksburg
Vidalia
Baton Rouge
New Orleans
LOUISIANA
Frankfort
KENTUCKY
Louisville
Knoxville
Nash-ville
TENN.
Memphis
ARKANSAS
MISSOURI
Mississippi

CUBA
Havana

1808-1860 250,000 slaves brought illegally to U.S.A. from Africa and the West Indies

TEXAS
Madisonville
Galveston
Matagorda
Port Lavaca

NEBRASKA TERRITORY

KANSAS TERRITORY

UTAH TERRITORY

NEW MEXICO TERRITORY

300
0
Miles

Slave States. By 1860 there were 4 million slaves in a southern population of 12 million

Territories opened to slavery by the Compromise of 1850

Territories closed to slavery by the Missouri Compromise of 1820, but opened to slavery by the Kansas-Nebraska Act of 1854

The domestic slave trade to 1860

52

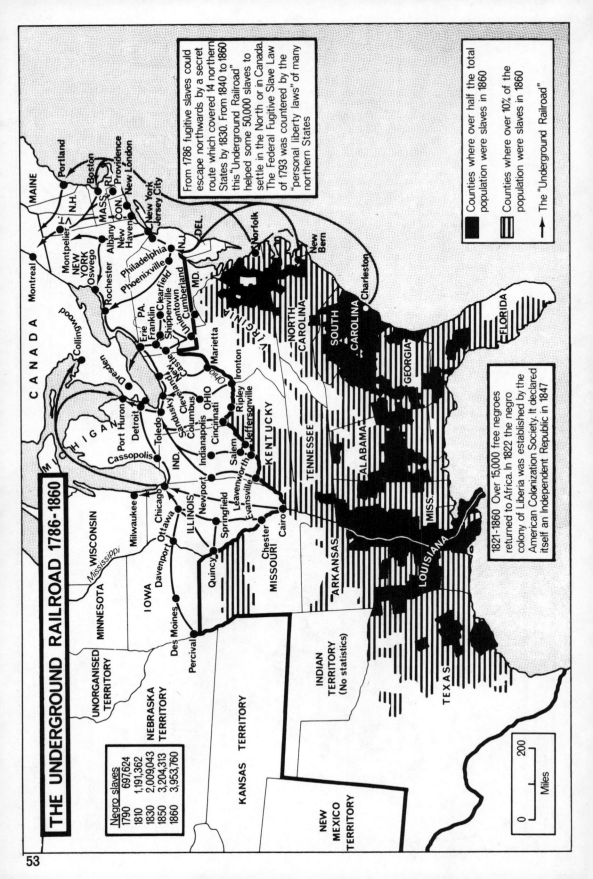

THE UNDERGROUND RAILROAD 1786-1860

Negro slaves	
1790	697,624
1810	1,191,362
1830	2,009,043
1850	3,204,313
1860	3,953,760

From 1786 fugitive slaves could escape northwards by a secret route which covered 14 northern States by 1830. This "Underground Railroad" helped some 50,000 slaves to settle in the North or in Canada. The Federal Fugitive Slave Law of 1793 was countered by the "personal liberty laws" of many northern States

1821-1860 Over 15,000 free negroes returned to Africa. In 1822 the negro colony of Liberia was established by the American Colonization Society. It declared itself an Independent Republic in 1847

Counties where over half the total population were slaves in 1860

Counties where over 10% of the population were slaves in 1860

The "Underground Railroad"

Miles
0   200

53

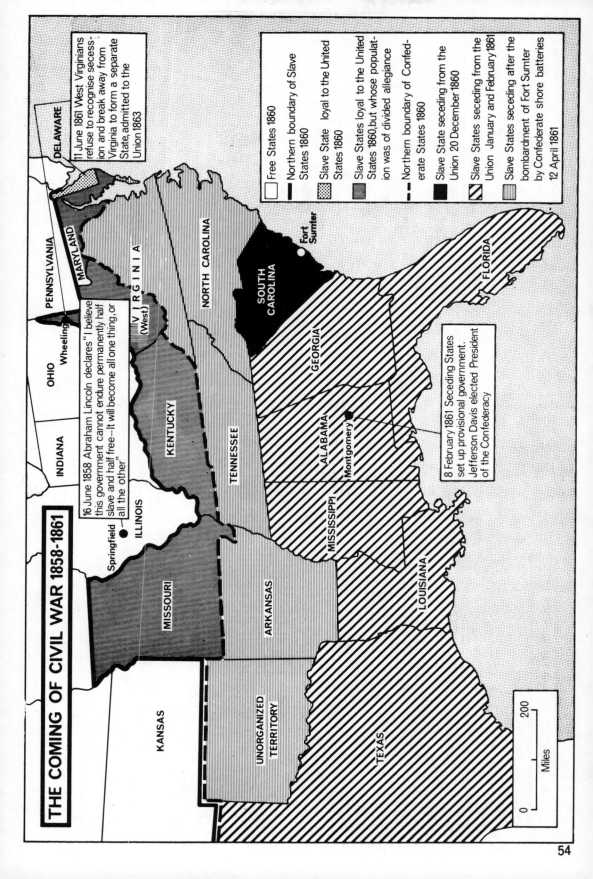

THE COMING OF CIVIL WAR 1858-1861

11 June 1861 West Virginians refuse to recognise secession and break away from Virginia to form a separate State, admitted to the Union 1863

DELAWARE

PENNSYLVANIA

MARYLAND

OHIO

Wheeling

VIRGINIA (West)

VIRGINIA

NORTH CAROLINA

Fort Sumter

SOUTH CAROLINA

16 June 1858 Abraham Lincoln declares "I believe this government cannot endure permanently half slave and half free...it will become all one thing, or all the other"

INDIANA

ILLINOIS

Springfield

KENTUCKY

TENNESSEE

GEORGIA

ALABAMA

Montgomery

MISSISSIPPI

8 February 1861 Seceding States set up provisional government. Jefferson Davis elected President of the Confederacy

MISSOURI

KANSAS

ARKANSAS

UNORGANIZED TERRITORY

LOUISIANA

TEXAS

FLORIDA

☐ Free States 1860

▮ Northern boundary of Slave States 1860

▨ Slave State loyal to the United States 1860

▦ Slave States loyal to the United States 1860, but whose population was of divided allegiance

▬ Northern boundary of Confederate States 1860

◼ Slave State seceding from the Union 20 December 1860

▨ Slave States seceding from the Union January and February 1861

▨ Slave States seceding after the bombardment of Fort Sumter by Confederate shore batteries 12 April 1861

0   200
|———————|
Miles

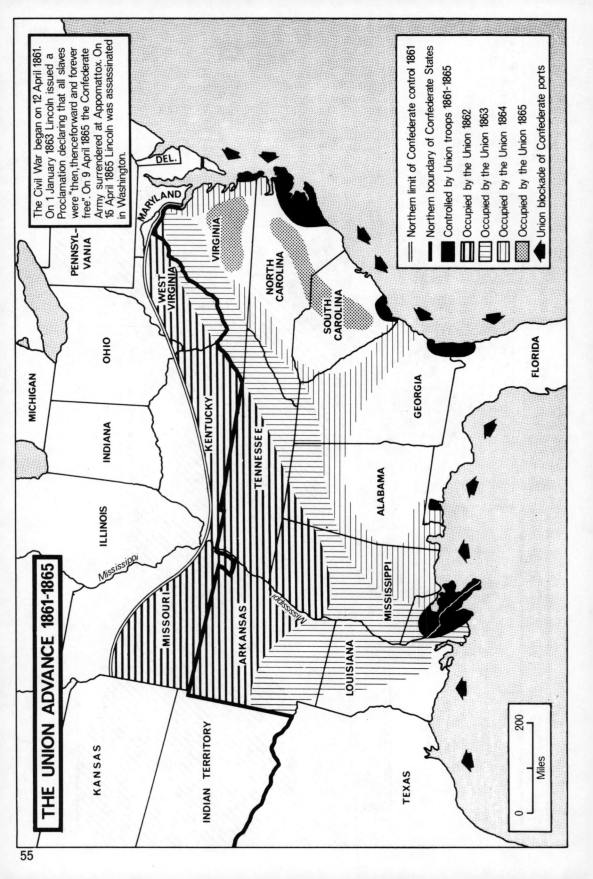

THE UNION ADVANCE 1861-1865

The Civil War began on 12 April 1861. On 1 January 1863 Lincoln issued a Proclamation declaring that all slaves were "then, thenceforward and forever free." On 9 April 1865 the Confederate Army surrendered at Appomattox. On 15 April 1865 Lincoln was assassinated in Washington.

Northern limit of Confederate control 1861
Northern boundary of Confederate States
Controlled by Union troops 1861-1865
Occupied by the Union 1862
Occupied by the Union 1863
Occupied by the Union 1864
Occupied by the Union 1865
Union blockade of Confederate ports

MICHIGAN
PENNSYLVANIA
DEL.
MARYLAND
WEST VIRGINIA
VIRGINIA
NORTH CAROLINA
SOUTH CAROLINA
OHIO
INDIANA
ILLINOIS
KENTUCKY
TENNESSEE
GEORGIA
ALABAMA
MISSISSIPPI
Mississippi
MISSOURI
ARKANSAS
LOUISIANA
KANSAS
INDIAN TERRITORY
TEXAS
FLORIDA

0   200
Miles

55

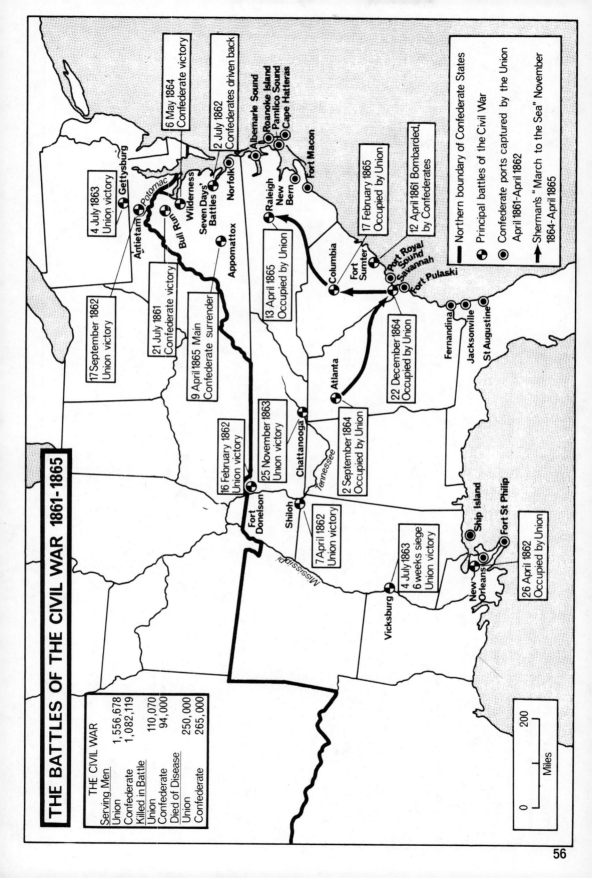

THE BATTLES OF THE CIVIL WAR 1861-1865

THE CIVIL WAR

Serving Men
Union 1,556,678
Confederate 1,082,119

Killed in Battle
Union 110,070
Confederate 94,000

Died of Disease
Union 250,000
Confederate 265,000

—— Northern boundary of Confederate States

● Principal battles of the Civil War

◉ Confederate ports captured by the Union April 1861-April 1862

→ Shermans "March to the Sea" November 1864-April 1865

6 May 1864 Confederate victory

2 July 1862 Confederates driven back

Albemarle Sound
Roanoke Island
Pamlico Sound
Cape Hatteras

Fort Macon

4 July 1863 Union victory

Gettysburg

Antietam

Bull Run

Wilderness

Seven Days' Battles

Norfolk

Raleigh

New Bern

Appomattox

17 September 1862 Union victory

21 July 1861 Confederate victory

9 April 1865 Main Confederate surrender

13 April 1865 Occupied by Union

Columbia

Fort Sumter

17 February 1865 Occupied by Union

12 April 1861 Bombarded, by Confederates

Fort Royal Sound
Savannah

Fort Pulaski

Fernandina

Jacksonville

St Augustine

16 February 1862 Union victory

25 November 1863 Union victory

Chattanooga

Tennessee

Fort Donelson

Shiloh

7 April 1862 Union victory

2 September 1864 Occupied by Union

Atlanta

22 December 1864 Occupied by Union

4 July 1863 6 weeks siege Union victory

Vicksburg

Mississippi

Ship Island

Fort St Philip

New Orleans

26 April 1862 Occupied by Union

Potomac

0   200
Miles

56

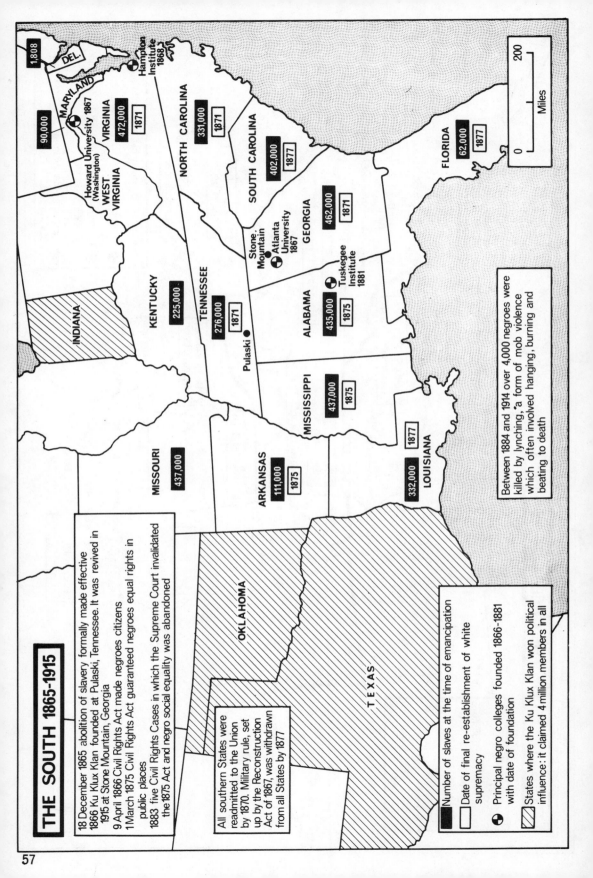

THE SOUTH 1865-1915

18 December 1865 abolition of slavery formally made effective
1866 Ku Klux Klan founded at Pulaski, Tennessee. It was revived in 1915 at Stone Mountain, Georgia
9 April 1866 Civil Rights Act made negroes citizens
1 March 1875 Civil Rights Act guaranteed negroes equal rights in public places
1883 five Civil Rights Cases in which the Supreme Court invalidated the 1875 Act and negro social equality was abandoned

All southern States were readmitted to the Union by 1870. Military rule, set up by the Reconstruction Act of 1867, was withdrawn from all States by 1877

Between 1884 and 1914 over 4,000 negroes were killed by lynching, a form of mob violence which often involved hanging, burning and beating to death

■ Number of slaves at the time of emancipation

□ Date of final re-establishment of white supremacy

◑ Principal negro colleges founded 1866-1881 with date of foundation

▨ States where the Ku Klux Klan won political influence: it claimed 4 million members in all

DEL.
1,808

MARYLAND
90,000

Hampton Institute 1868

Howard University 1867 (Washington)

WEST VIRGINIA

VIRGINIA
472,000 | 1871

NORTH CAROLINA
331,000 | 1871

SOUTH CAROLINA
402,000 | 1877

GEORGIA
462,000 | 1871

FLORIDA
62,000 | 1877

Stone Mountain

Atlanta University 1867

Tuskegee Institute 1881

ALABAMA
435,000 | 1875

KENTUCKY
225,000

INDIANA

TENNESSEE
276,000 | 1871

Pulaski

MISSISSIPPI
437,000 | 1875

MISSOURI
437,000

ARKANSAS
111,000 | 1875

LOUISIANA
332,000 | 1877

OKLAHOMA

TEXAS

0   200
Miles

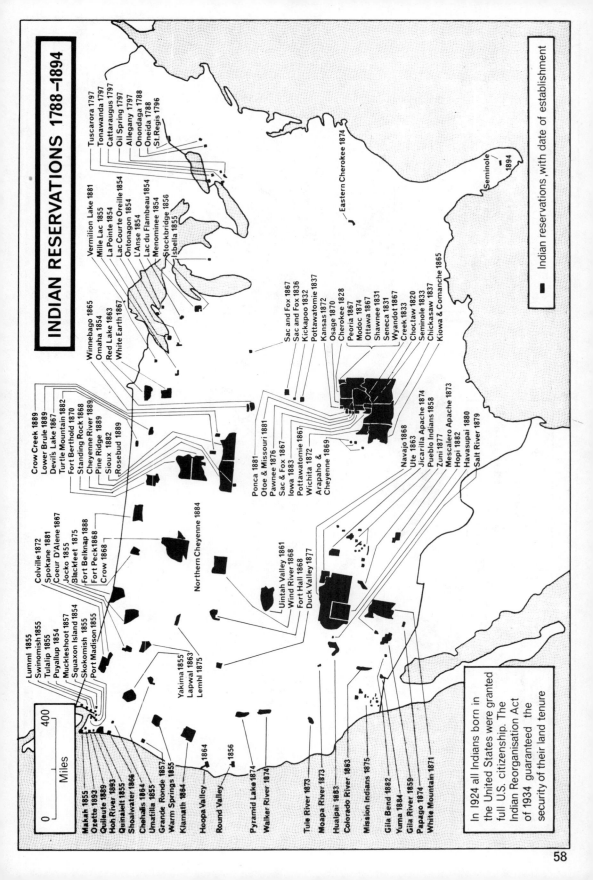

INDIAN RESERVATIONS 1788–1894

Indian reservations, with date of establishment

Tuscarora 1797
Tonawanda 1797
Cattaraugus 1797
Oil Spring 1797
Allegany 1797
Onondaga 1788
Oneida 1788
St. Regis 1796

Eastern Cherokee 1874

Seminole 1894

Vermilion Lake 1881
Mille Lac 1855
La Pointe 1854
Lac Courte Oreille 1854
Ontonagon 1854
L'Anse 1854
Lac du Flambeau 1854
Menominee 1854
Stockbridge 1856
Isbella 1855

Winnebago 1865
Omaha 1854
Red Lake 1863
White Earth 1867

Sac and Fox 1867
Sac and Fox 1836
Kickapoo 1832
Pottawatomie 1837
Kansas 1872
Osage 1870
Cherokee 1828
Peoria 1867
Modoc 1874
Ottawa 1867
Shawnee 1831
Seneca 1831
Wyandot 1867
Creek 1833
Choctaw 1820
Seminole 1833
Chickasaw 1837
Kiowa & Comanche 1865

Crow Creek 1889
Lower Brule 1889
Devil's Lake 1867
Turtle Mountain 1882
Fort Berthold 1870
Standing Rock 1868
Cheyenne River 1889
Pine Ridge 1889
Sioux 1889
Rosebud 1889

Ponca 1881
Otoe & Missouri 1881
Pawnee 1876
Sac & Fox 1867
Iowa 1883
Pottawatomie 1867
Wichita 1872
Arapaho &
Cheyenne 1869

Navajo 1868
Ute 1863
Jicarilla Apache 1874
Pueblo Indians 1858
Zuni 1877
Mescalero Apache 1873
Hopi 1882
Havasupai 1880
Salt River 1879

Colville 1872
Spokane 1881
Coeur D'Alene 1867
Jocko 1855
Blackfeet 1875
Fort Belknap 1888
Crow 1868

Northern Cheyenne 1884

Uintah Valley 1861
Wind River 1868
Fort Hall 1868
Duck Valley 1877

Lummi 1855
Swinomish 1855
Tulalip 1855
Puyallup 1854
Muckleshoot 1857
Squaxon Island 1854
Skokomish 1855
Port Madison 1855

Yakima 1855
Lapwai 1863
Lemhi 1875

Makah 1855
Ozette 1893
Quileute 1889
Hoh River 1893
Quinaielt 1855
Shoalwater 1866
Chehalis 1864
Umatilla 1855
Grande Ronde 1857
Warm Springs 1855
Klamath 1864

Hoopa Valley 1864

Round Valley 1856

Pyramid Lake 1874
Walker River 1874

Tule River 1873

Moapa River 1873

Hualpai 1883
Colorado River 1863

Mission Indians 1875

Gila Bend 1882
Yuma 1884
Gila River 1859
Papago 1874
White Mountain 1871

0	400
Miles	

In 1924 all Indians born in
the United States were granted
full U.S. citizenship. The
Indian Reorganisation Act
of 1934 guaranteed the
security of their land tenure

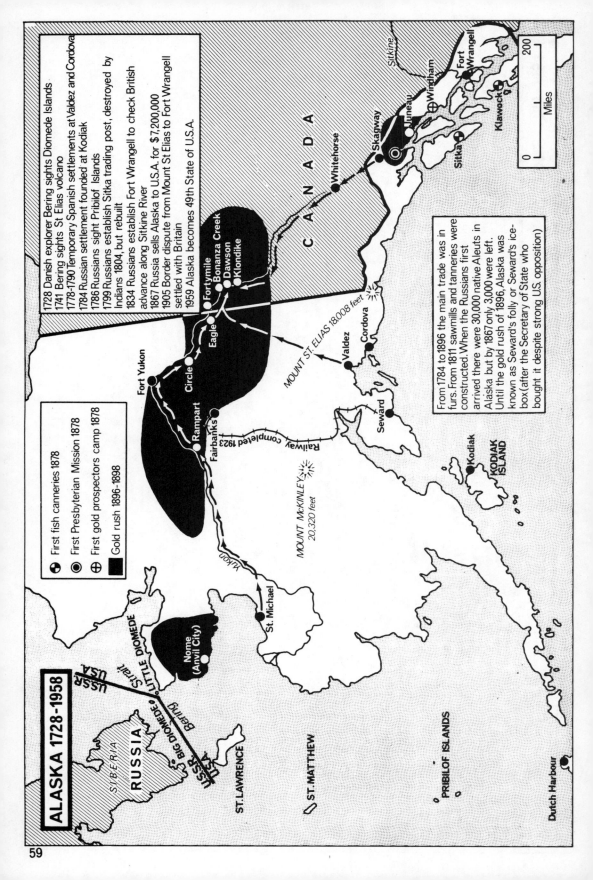

ALASKA 1728-1958

1728 Danish explorer Bering sights Diomede Islands
1741 Bering sights St Elias volcano
1778-1790 Temporary Spanish settlements at Valdez and Cordova
1784 Russian settlement founded at Kodiak
1786 Russians sight Pribilof Islands
1799 Russians establish Sitka trading post, destroyed by Indians 1804, but rebuilt
1834 Russians establish Fort Wrangell to check British advance along Sitkine River
1867 Russia sells Alaska to U.S.A. for $7,200,000
1905 Border dispute from Mount St Elias to Fort Wrangell settled with Britain
1959 Alaska becomes 49th State of U.S.A.

◑ First fish canneries 1878
◎ First Presbyterian Mission 1878
⊕ First gold prospectors camp 1878
■ Gold rush 1896-1898

From 1784 to 1896 the main trade was in furs. From 1811 sawmills and tanneries were constructed. When the Russians first arrived there were 30,000 native Aleuts in Alaska but by 1867 only 3,000 were left. Until the gold rush of 1896, Alaska was known as Seward's folly or Seward's ice-box (after the Secretary of State who bought it despite strong U.S. opposition)

RUSSIA

SIBERIA

USSR USA

Bering Strait

BIG DIOMEDE
LITTLE DIOMEDE

ST. LAWRENCE

ST. MATTHEW

PRIBILOF ISLANDS

Dutch Harbour

KODIAK ISLAND

Kodiak

Seward

Cordova

Valdez

MOUNT ST. ELIAS 18,008 feet

MOUNT McKINLEY 20,320 feet

St. Michael

Nome (Anvil City)

YUKON

Railway completed 1923

Fairbanks

Rampart

Circle

Fort Yukon

Eagle

Fortymile
Bonanza Creek
Dawson
Klondike

CANADA

Whitehorse

Skagway

Juneau

Windham

Fort Wrangell

Sitka

Klawock

Sitkine

Miles
0   200

59

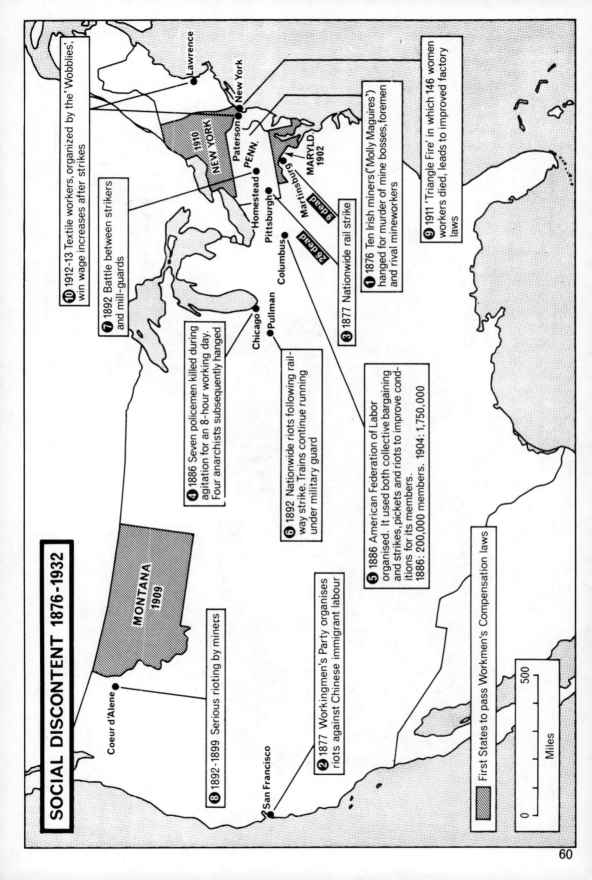

SOCIAL DISCONTENT 1876-1932

10 1912-13 Textile workers, organized by the 'Wobblies', win wage increases after strikes

7 1892 Battle between strikers and mill-guards

9 1911 'Triangle Fire' in which 146 women workers died, leads to improved factory laws

1 1876 Ten Irish miners ("Molly Maguires") hanged for murder of mine bosses, foremen and rival mineworkers

3 1877 Nationwide rail strike

4 1886 Seven policemen killed during agitation for an 8-hour working day. Four anarchists subsequently hanged

6 1892 Nationwide riots following railway strike. Trains continue running under military guard

5 1886 American Federation of Labor organised. It used both collective bargaining and strikes, pickets and riots to improve conditions for its members. 1886: 200,000 members. 1904: 1,750,000

8 1892-1899 Serious rioting by miners

2 1877 Workingmen's Party organises riots against Chinese immigrant labour

New York

Lawrence

1910 NEW YORK

Paterson
PENN.
MARYLD. 1902
Martinsburg
9 dead
Homestead
Pittsburgh
26 dead
Columbus

Pullman

Chicago

MONTANA 1909

Coeur d'Alene

San Francisco

First States to pass Workmen's Compensation laws

Miles
0   500

60

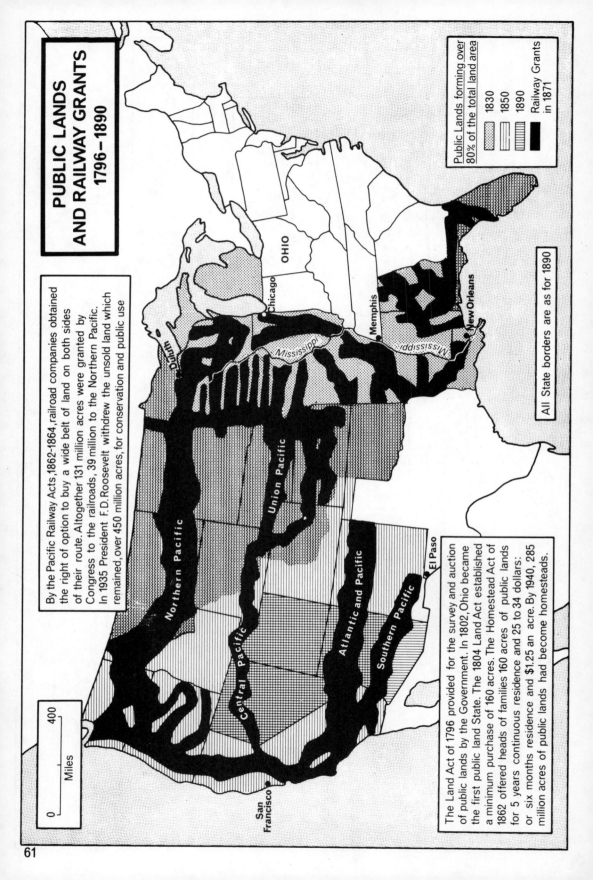

PUBLIC LANDS
AND RAILWAY GRANTS
1796–1890

By the Pacific Railway Acts,1862-1864, railroad companies obtained the right of option to buy a wide belt of land on both sides of their route. Altogether 131 million acres were granted by Congress to the railroads, 39 million to the Northern Pacific. In 1935 President F.D. Roosevelt withdrew the unsold land which remained, over 450 million acres, for conservation and public use

The Land Act of 1796 provided for the survey and auction of public lands by the Government. In 1802, Ohio became the first public land State. The 1804 Land Act established a minimum purchase of 160 acres. The Homestead Act of 1862 offered heads of families 160 acres of public lands for 5 years continuous residence and 25 to 34 dollars; or six months residence and $1.25 an acre. By 1940, 285 million acres of public lands had become homesteads.

Public Lands forming over 80% of the total land area

1830

1850

1890

Railway Grants in 1871

All State borders are as for 1890

400

Miles

0

San Francisco

OHIO

Chicago

Duluth

Mississippi

Memphis

Mississippi

New Orleans

Northern Pacific

Central Pacific

Union Pacific

Atlantic and Pacific

Southern Pacific

El Paso

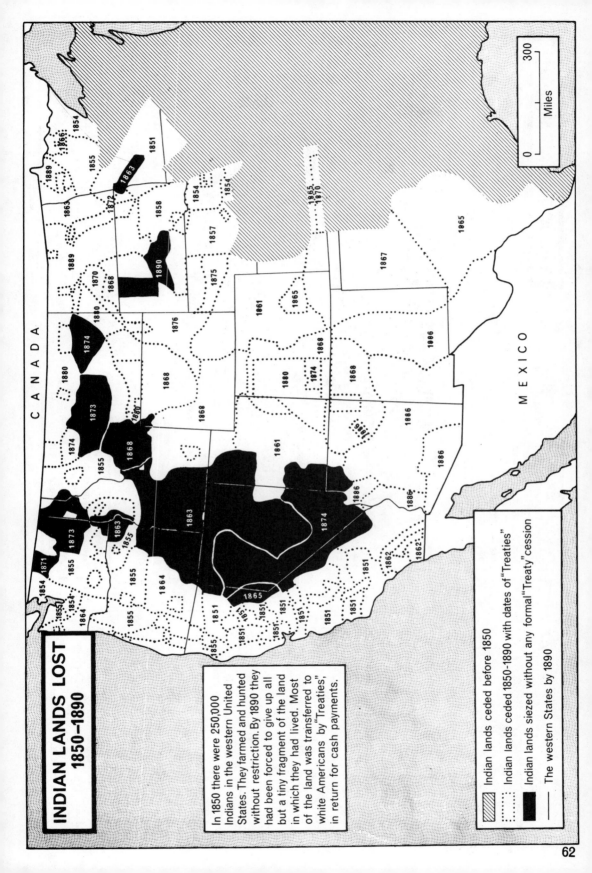

INDIAN LANDS LOST 1850–1890

In 1850 there were 250,000 Indians in the western United States. They farmed and hunted without restriction. By 1890 they had been forced to give up all but a tiny fragment of the land in which they had lived. Most of the land was transferred to white Americans by "Treaties," in return for cash payments.

CANADA

MEXICO

0   300

Miles

Indian lands ceded before 1850

Indian lands ceded 1850–1890 with dates of "Treaties"

Indian lands siezed without any formal "Treaty" cession

The western States by 1890

1854
1854
1855
1851
1889
1866
1863
1872
1863
1858
1854
1854
1857
1889
1870
1868
1875
1890
1876
1861
1865
1874
1880
1880
1868
1868
1868
1868
1876
1873
1880
1855
1874
1874
1861
1880
1874
1868
1855
1873
1863
1855
1863
1864
1865
1870
1867
1866
1886
1886
1886
1886
1886
1871
1854
1851
1854
1864
1855
1855
1855
1864
1851
1851
1851
1851
1851
1851
1851
1851
1851
1851
1855
1862
1862
1886
1886
1874

62

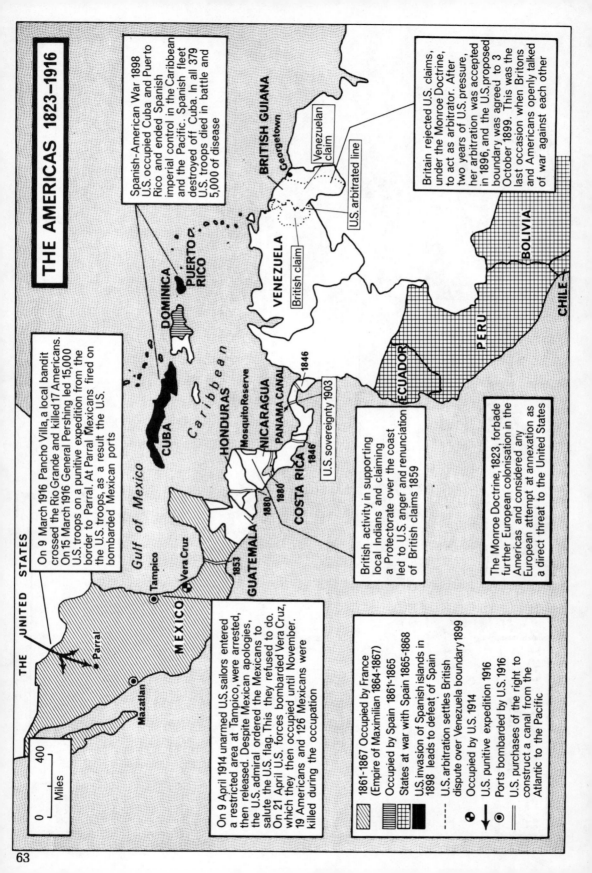

THE AMERICAS 1823–1916

THE UNITED STATES

MEXICO

Mazatlan
Tampico
Vera Cruz
Parral

Gulf of Mexico

GUATEMALA
1853
HONDURAS
Mosquito Reserve
NICARAGUA
1880
PANAMA CANAL
1880
COSTA RICA
1846

CUBA
DOMINICA
PUERTO RICO

Caribbean

BRITISH GUIANA
Georgetown

VENEZUELA
British claim
Venezuelan claim
U.S. arbitrated line
1846

ECUADOR
PERU
BOLIVIA
CHILE

0   400
Miles

Spanish-American War 1898 U.S. occupied Cuba and Puerto Rico and ended Spanish imperial control in the Caribbean and the Pacific. Spanish fleet destroyed off Cuba. In all 379 U.S. troops died in battle and 5,000 of disease

Britain rejected U.S. claims, under the Monroe Doctrine, to act as arbitrator. After two years of U.S. pressure, her arbitration was accepted in 1896, and the U.S. proposed boundary was agreed to 3 October 1899. This was the last occasion when Britons and Americans openly talked of war against each other

On 9 March 1916 Pancho Villa, a local bandit crossed the Rio Grande and killed 17 Americans. On 15 March 1916 General Pershing led 15,000 U.S. troops on a punitive expedition from the border to Parral. At Parral Mexicans fired on the U.S. troops, as a result the U.S. bombarded Mexican ports

On 9 April 1914 unarmed U.S. sailors entered a restricted area at Tampico, were arrested, then released. Despite Mexican apologies, the U.S. admiral ordered the Mexicans to salute the U.S. flag. This they refused to do. On 21 April U.S. forces bombarded Vera Cruz, which they then occupied until November. 19 Americans and 126 Mexicans were killed during the occupation

British activity in supporting local Indians and claiming a Protectorate over the coast led to U.S. anger and renunciation of British claims 1859

U.S. sovereignty 1903

The Monroe Doctrine, 1823, forbade further European colonisation in the Americas and considered any European attempt at annexation as a direct threat to the United States

1861-1867 Occupied by France
(Empire of Maximilian 1864-1867)

Occupied by Spain 1861-1865

States at war with Spain 1865-1868

U.S. invasion of Spanish islands in 1898 leads to defeat of Spain

U.S. arbitration settles British dispute over Venezuela boundary 1899

Occupied by U.S. 1914

U.S. punitive expedition 1916

Ports bombarded by U.S. 1916

U.S. purchases of the right to construct a canal from the Atlantic to the Pacific

63

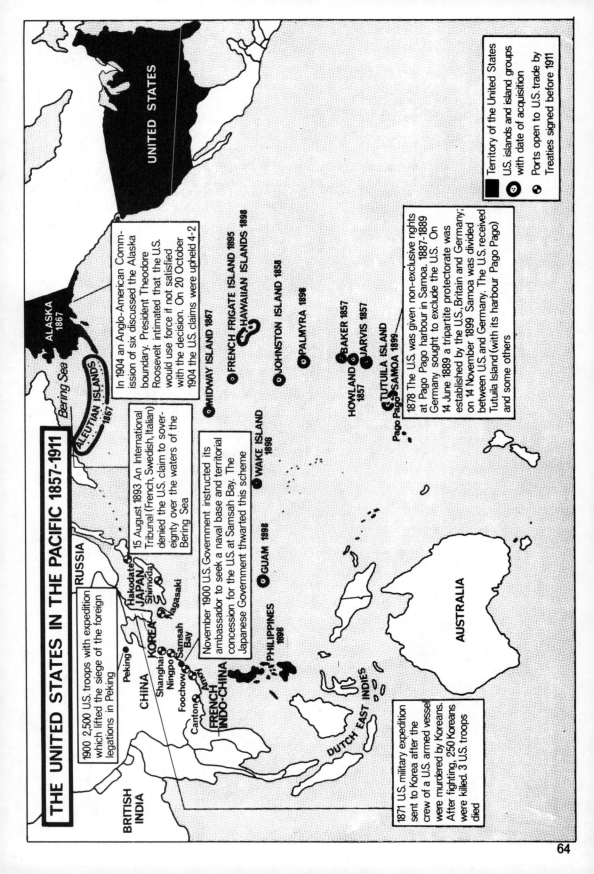

THE UNITED STATES IN THE PACIFIC 1857-1911

UNITED STATES

ALASKA 1867

Bering Sea

ALEUTIAN ISLANDS 1867

RUSSIA

BRITISH INDIA

CHINA

Peking ●

JAPAN
Hakodate ●
Shimoda ●
Nagasaki ●

KOREA ●

Shanghai ●
Ningpo ●
Foochow ●
Samsah Bay
Canton ●
Amoy ●
FRENCH INDO-CHINA

PHILIPPINES 1898

GUAM 1898

WAKE ISLAND 1898

DUTCH EAST INDIES

AUSTRALIA

MIDWAY ISLAND 1867

FRENCH FRIGATE ISLAND 1895

HAWAIIAN ISLANDS 1898

JOHNSTON ISLAND 1858

PALMYRA 1898

HOWLAND 1857

BAKER 1857

JARVIS 1857

TUTUILA ISLAND
Pago Pago SAMOA 1899

1900 2,500 U.S. troops with expedition which lifted the siege of the foreign legations in Peking

In 1904 an Anglo-American Commission of six discussed the Alaska boundary. President Theodore Roosevelt intimated that the U.S. would use force if not satisfied with the decision. On 20 October 1904 the U.S. claims were upheld 4-2

15 August 1893 An International Tribunal (French, Swedish, Italian) denied the U.S. claim to sovereignty over the waters of the Bering Sea

November 1900 U.S. Government instructed its ambassador to seek a naval base and territorial concession for the U.S. at Samsah Bay. The Japanese Government thwarted this scheme

1878 The U.S. was given non-exclusive rights at Pago Pago harbour in Samoa. 1887-1889 Germany sought to exclude the U.S. On 14 June 1889 a tripartite protectorate was established by the U.S., Britain and Germany; on 14 November 1899 Samoa was divided between U.S. and Germany. The U.S. received Tutuila Island (with its harbour Pago Pago) and some others

1871 U.S. military expedition sent to Korea after the crew of a U.S. armed vessel were murdered by Koreans. After fighting, 250 Koreans were killed. 3 U.S. troops died

Territory of the United States

U.S. islands and island groups with date of acquisition

Ports open to U.S. trade by Treaties signed before 1911

64

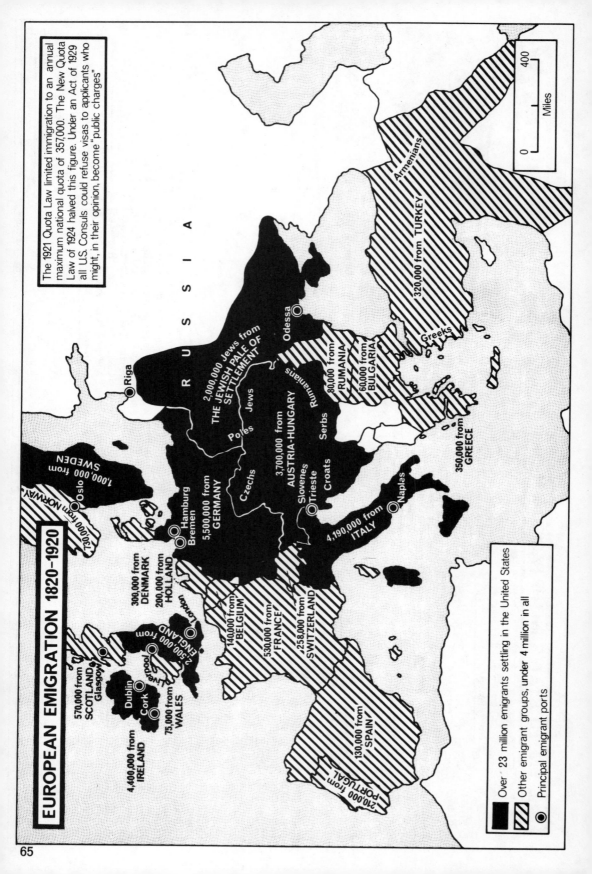

EUROPEAN EMIGRATION 1820-1920

The 1921 Quota Law limited immigration to an annual maximum national quota of 357,000. The New Quota Law of 1924 halved this figure. Under an Act of 1929 all U.S. Consuls could refuse visas to applicants who might, in their opinion, become "public charges"

RUSSIA

2,000,000 Jews from THE JEWISH PALE OF SETTLEMENT

Jews

Poles

Czechs

AUSTRIA-HUNGARY

Slovenes

Rumanians

Serbs

Croats

3,700,000 from

5,500,000 from GERMANY

SWEDEN
1,000,000 from

NORWAY
730,000 from

Oslo

Riga

Odessa

80,000 from RUMANIA

60,000 from BULGARIA

Greeks

350,000 from GREECE

320,000 from TURKEY

Armenians

Hamburg
Bremen

300,000 from DENMARK

200,000 from HOLLAND

140,000 from BELGIUM

530,000 from FRANCE

258,000 from SWITZERLAND

4,190,000 from ITALY

Trieste

Naples

130,000 from SPAIN

210,000 from PORTUGAL

570,000 from SCOTLAND

Glasgow

IRELAND
4,400,000 from

Dublin

Cork

Liverpool

London

ENGLAND
2,500,000 from

75,000 from WALES

Miles
0   400

■ Over 23 million emigrants settling in the United States

▨ Other emigrant groups, under 4 million in all

◉ Principal emigrant ports

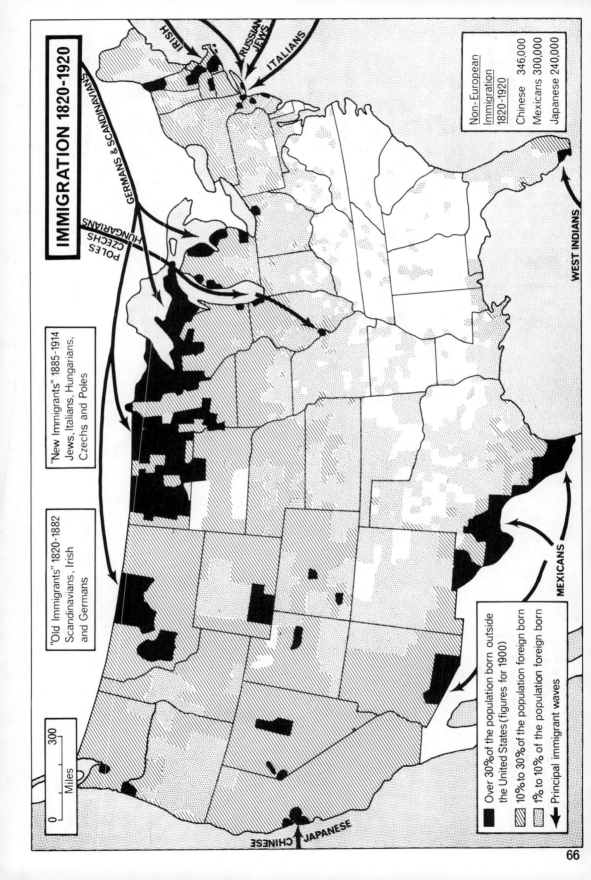

IMMIGRATION 1820-1920

Non-European
Immigration
1820-1920

Chinese   346,000
Mexicans   300,000
Japanese   240,000

RUSSIAN
JEWS

IRISH

ITALIANS

GERMANS & SCANDINAVIANS

POLES
CZECHS
HUNGARIANS

WEST INDIANS

MEXICANS

CHINESE   JAPANESE

"New Immigrants" 1885-1914
Jews, Italians, Hungarians,
Czechs and Poles

"Old Immigrants" 1820-1882
Scandinavians, Irish
and Germans

300

0   Miles

Over 30% of the population born outside
the United States (figures for 1900)

10% to 30% of the population foreign born

1% to 10% of the population foreign born

Principal immigrant waves

66

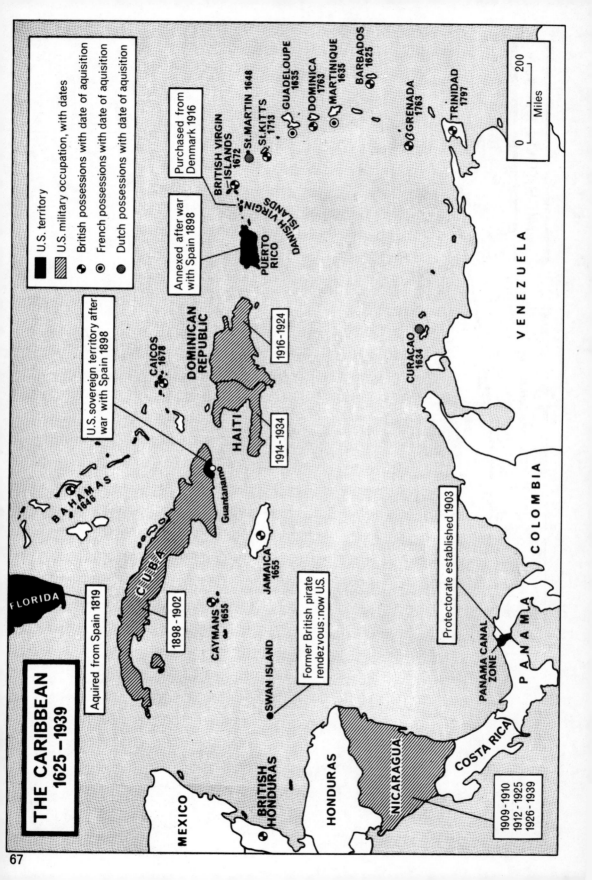

THE CARIBBEAN 1625–1939

Legend:
- ■ U.S. territory
- ▨ U.S. military occupation, with dates
- ◐ British possessions with date of aquisition
- ◉ French possessions with date of aquisition
- ◑ Dutch possessions with date of aquisition

Aquired from Spain 1819 — FLORIDA

U.S. sovereign territory after war with Spain 1898

Purchased from Denmark 1916

Annexed after war with Spain 1898 — PUERTO RICO

BRITISH VIRGIN ISLANDS 1672

DANISH VIRGIN ISLANDS

St. MARTIN 1648

St. KITTS 1713

GUADELOUPE 1635

DOMINICA 1763

MARTINIQUE 1635

BARBADOS 1625

GRENADA 1763

TRINIDAD 1797

CAICOS 1678

BAHAMAS 1646

DOMINICAN REPUBLIC 1916–1924

HAITI 1914–1934

CUBA 1898–1902

Guantanamo

JAMAICA 1655

CAYMANS 1655

Former British pirate rendezvous : now U.S.

SWAN ISLAND

CURACAO 1634

Protectorate established 1903

PANAMA CANAL ZONE

MEXICO

BRITISH HONDURAS

HONDURAS

NICARAGUA
1909–1910
1912–1925
1926–1939

COSTA RICA

PANAMA

COLOMBIA

VENEZUELA

0   200
Miles

67

THE PANAMA CANAL ZONE PROTECTORATE 1903

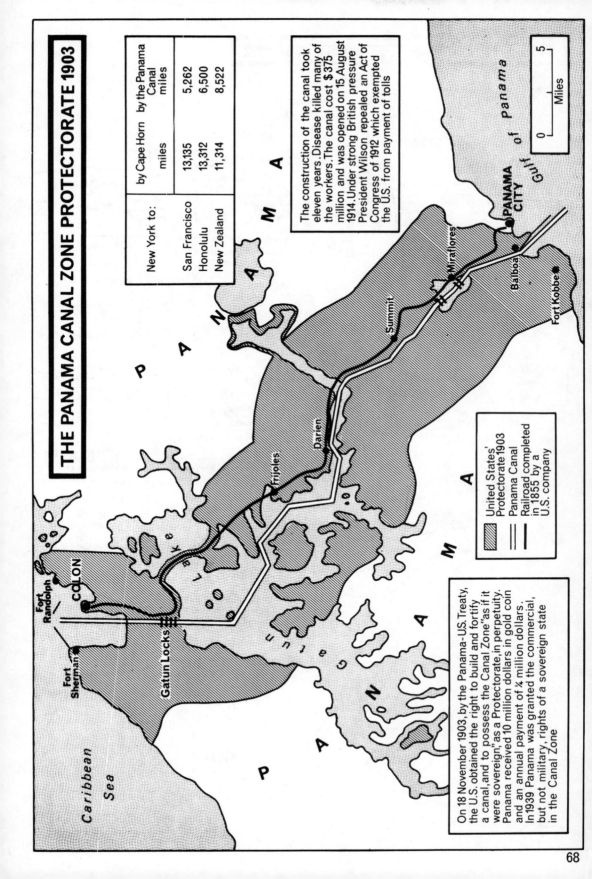

New York to:	by Cape Horn miles	by the Panama Canal miles
San Francisco	13,135	5,262
Honolulu	13,312	6,500
New Zealand	11,314	8,522

The construction of the canal took eleven years. Disease killed many of the workers. The canal cost $375 million and was opened on 15 August 1914. Under strong British pressure President Wilson repealed an Act of Congress of 1912 which exempted the U.S. from payment of tolls

GULF of Panama

0   5
Miles

PANAMA CITY
Miraflores
Summit
Balboa
Fort Kobbe

Darien
Frijoles

P A N A M A

United
Fort Sherman
COLON
Fort Randolph
Gatun Locks

Caribbean Sea

United States' Protectorate 1903
Panama Canal
Railroad completed in 1855 by a U.S. company

On 18 November 1903, by the Panama–U.S. Treaty, the U.S. obtained the right to build and fortify a canal, and to possess the Canal Zone "as if it were sovereign," as a Protectorate, in perpetuity. Panama received 10 million dollars in gold coin and an annual payment of ¼ million dollars. In 1939 Panama was granted the commercial, but not military, rights of a sovereign state in the Canal Zone

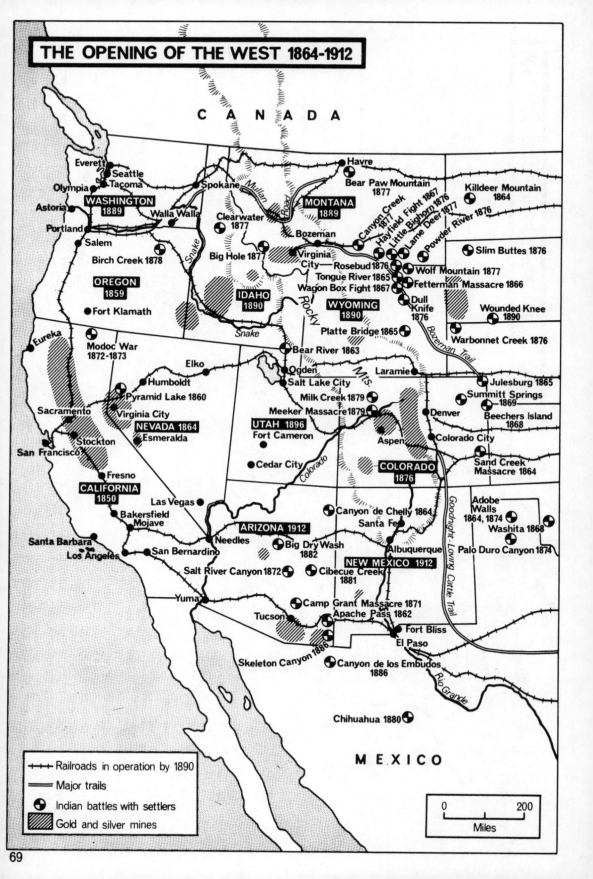

THE OPENING OF THE WEST 1864-1912

C A N A D A

Everett
Seattle
Olympia · Tacoma
Astoria
Portland
Salem
WASHINGTON 1889
Walla Walla
Spokane
Mullan Road

Havre
Bear Paw Mountain 1877
Killdeer Mountain 1864

Clearwater 1877
Bozeman
MONTANA 1889
Canyon Creek 1877
Hayfield Fight 1867
Little Bighorn 1876
Lame Deer 1877
Powder River 1876
Slim Buttes 1876

Birch Creek 1878
Big Hole 1877
Virginia City
Rosebud 1876
Tongue River 1865
Wagon Box Fight 1867
Wolf Mountain 1877
Fetterman Massacre 1866

OREGON 1859
IDAHO 1890
Rocky
WYOMING 1890
Dull Knife 1876
Wounded Knee 1890

Fort Klamath
Snake
Platte Bridge 1865
Bozeman Trail
Warbonnet Creek 1876

Eureka
Bear River 1863
Ogden
Laramie
Julesburg 1865

Modoc War 1872-1873
Elko
Salt Lake City
Milk Creek 1879
Mts.
Summitt Springs 1869
Beechers Island 1868

Humboldt
Meeker Massacre 1879
Denver

Sacramento
Pyramid Lake 1860
Virginia City
NEVADA 1864
Esmeralda
UTAH 1896
Fort Cameron
Aspen
Colorado City

Stockton
San Francisco
Cedar City
Colorado
COLORADO 1876
Sand Creek Massacre 1864

Fresno
CALIFORNIA 1850
Las Vegas

Bakersfield
Mojave
Canyon de Chelly 1864
Santa Fe
Adobe Walls 1864, 1874
Washita 1868

Santa Barbara
Los Angeles
San Bernardino
Needles
ARIZONA 1912
Big Dry Wash 1882
NEW MEXICO 1912
Albuquerque
Palo Duro Canyon 1874
Goodnight-Loving Cattle Trail

Salt River Canyon 1872
Cibecue Creek 1881

Yuma
Camp Grant Massacre 1871
Apache Pass 1862
Tucson
Fort Bliss
El Paso

Skeleton Canyon 1886
Canyon de los Embudos 1886
Rio Grande

Chihuahua 1880

M E X I C O

+++ Railroads in operation by 1890
— Major trails
⊕ Indian battles with settlers
▨ Gold and silver mines

0 — 200
Miles

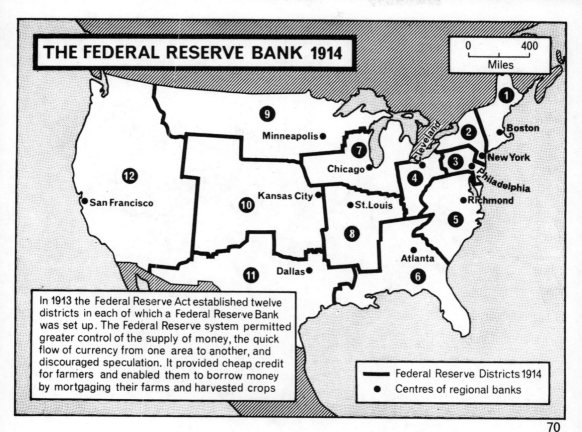

THE FEDERAL RESERVE BANK 1914

0   400
Miles

⑨   Minneapolis ●

⑦

Cleveland

① Boston

② New York

③ Philadelphia

Chicago

④

Kansas City ●

⑩

St. Louis ●

Richmond

⑤

⑫ San Francisco ●

⑧

⑪ Dallas ●

Atlanta

⑥

In 1913 the Federal Reserve Act established twelve districts in each of which a Federal Reserve Bank was set up. The Federal Reserve system permitted greater control of the supply of money, the quick flow of currency from one area to another, and discouraged speculation. It provided cheap credit for farmers and enabled them to borrow money by mortgaging their farms and harvested crops

—— Federal Reserve Districts 1914
● Centres of regional banks

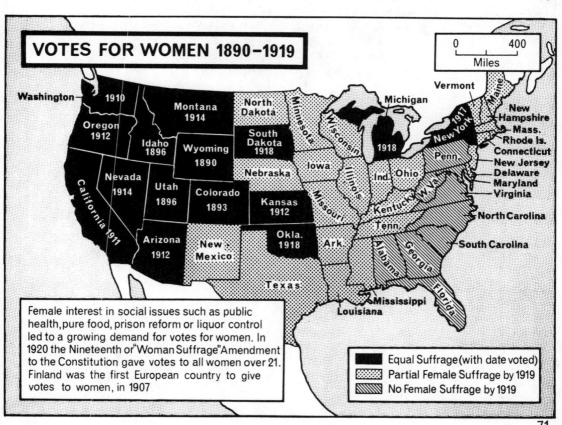

VOTES FOR WOMEN 1890-1919

0   400
Miles

Washington — 1910

Montana 1914

North Dakota

Michigan

Vermont

Maine

New Hampshire

Oregon 1912

Idaho 1896

Wyoming 1890

South Dakota 1918

Wisconsin

Minnesota

1918

New York 1917

Mass.

Rhode Is.

Connecticut

Nevada 1914

Utah 1896

Colorado 1893

Nebraska

Iowa

Illinois

Ind.

Ohio

Penn.

New Jersey

Delaware

Maryland

Virginia

W.Va.

Kentucky

California 1911

Arizona 1912

New Mexico

Okla. 1918

Kansas 1912

Missouri

Tenn.

North Carolina

Ark.

Alabama

Georgia

South Carolina

Texas

Mississippi

Louisiana

Florida

Female interest in social issues such as public health, pure food, prison reform or liquor control led to a growing demand for votes for women. In 1920 the Nineteenth or "Woman Suffrage" Amendment to the Constitution gave votes to all women over 21. Finland was the first European country to give votes to women, in 1907

▮ Equal Suffrage (with date voted)
▨ Partial Female Suffrage by 1919
▧ No Female Suffrage by 1919

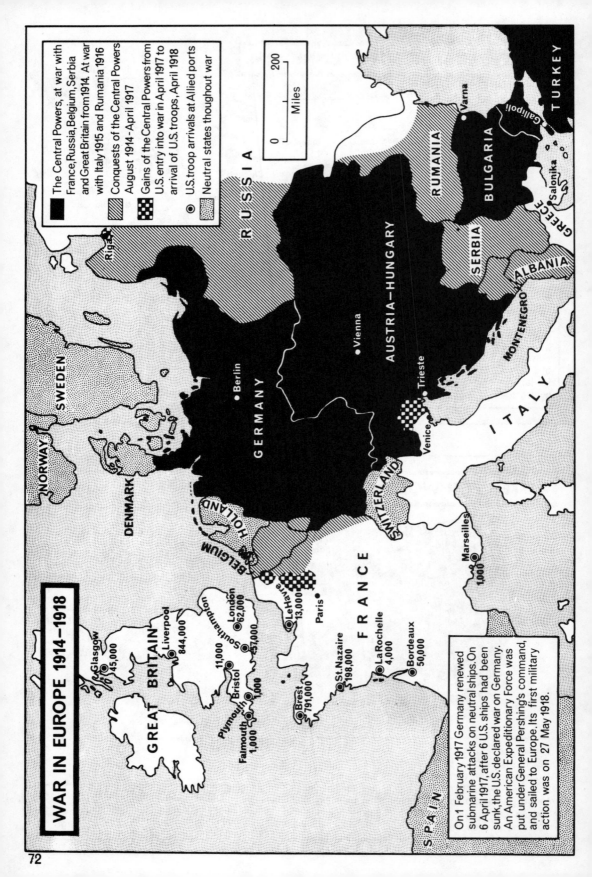

WAR IN EUROPE 1914–1918

The Central Powers, at war with France, Russia, Belgium, Serbia and Great Britain from 1914. At war with Italy 1915 and Rumania 1916

Conquests of the Central Powers August 1914 - April 1917

Gains of the Central Powers from U.S. entry into war in April 1917 to arrival of U.S. troops, April 1918

⊙ U.S. troop arrivals at Allied ports

Neutral states thoughout war

0   200
Miles

On 1 February 1917 Germany renewed submarine attacks on neutral ships. On 6 April 1917, after 6 U.S. ships had been sunk, the U.S. declared war on Germany. An American Expeditionary Force was put under General Pershing's command, and sailed to Europe. Its first military action was on 27 May 1918.

72

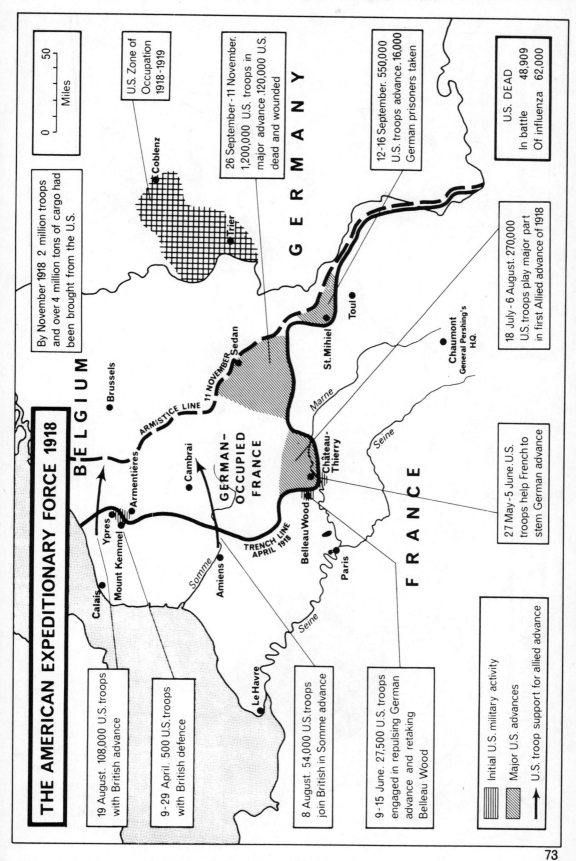

THE AMERICAN EXPEDITIONARY FORCE 1918

BELGIUM

GERMANY

FRANCE

GERMAN-OCCUPIED FRANCE

U.S. Zone of Occupation 1918-1919

26 September - 11 November. 1,200,000 U.S. troops in major advance. 120,000 U.S. dead and wounded

12-16 September. 550,000 U.S. troops advance. 16,000 German prisoners taken

U.S. DEAD
In battle 48,909
Of influenza 62,000

By November 1918 2 million troops and over 4 million tons of cargo had been brought from the U.S.

18 July - 6 August. 270,000 U.S. troops play major part in first Allied advance of 1918

27 May - 5 June. U.S. troops help French to stem German advance

19 August. 108,000 U.S. troops with British advance

9-29 April. 500 U.S. troops with British defence

8 August. 54,000 U.S. troops join British in Somme advance

9-15 June. 27,500 U.S. troops engaged in repulsing German advance and retaking Belleau Wood

Initial U.S. military activity

Major U.S. advances

U.S. troop support for allied advance

ARMISTICE LINE 11 NOVEMBER

TRENCH LINE APRIL 1918

Coblenz

Trier

Brussels

Armentières

Cambrai

Sedan

St. Mihiel

Toul

Chaumont
General Pershing's H.Q.

Château-Thierry

Belleau Wood

Paris

Ypres

Mount Kemmel

Calais

Amiens

Le Havre

Somme

Seine

Seine

Marne

50
Miles
0

73

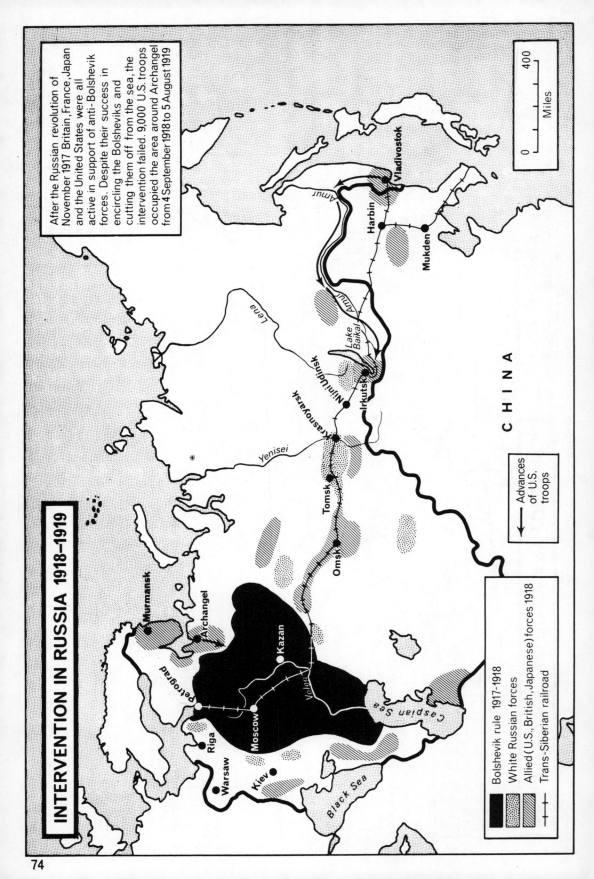

INTERVENTION IN RUSSIA 1918–1919

After the Russian revolution of November 1917 Britain, France, Japan and the United States were all active in support of anti-Bolshevik forces. Despite their success in encircling the Bolsheviks and cutting them off from the sea, the intervention failed. 9,000 U.S. troops occupied the area around Archangel from 4 September 1918 to 5 August 1919

0   400

Miles

Vladivostok

Harbin

Mukden

C H I N A

Amur

Amur

Lena

Lake Baikal

NizhUdinsk

Irkutsk

Krasnoyarsk

Yenisei

Tomsk

Omsk

Murmansk

Archangel

Kazan

Petrograd

Volga

Moscow

Riga

Warsaw

Kiev

Caspian Sea

Black Sea

Advances of U.S. troops

Bolshevik rule 1917–1918

White Russian forces

Allied (U.S., British, Japanese) forces 1918

Trans-Siberian railroad

74

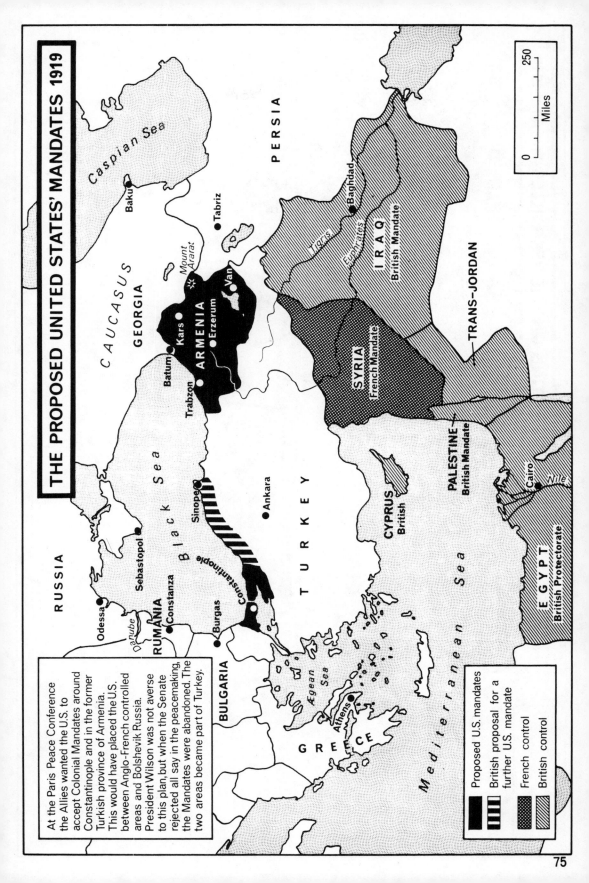

THE PROPOSED UNITED STATES' MANDATES 1919

At the Paris Peace Conference the Allies wanted the U.S. to accept Colonial Mandates around Constantinople and in the former Turkish province of Armenia. This would have placed the U.S. between Anglo-French controlled areas and Bolshevik Russia. President Wilson was not averse to this plan, but when the Senate rejected all say in the peacemaking, the Mandates were abandoned. The two areas became part of Turkey.

250

0   Miles

PERSIA

Caspian Sea

Baku

Tabriz

Baghdad

Euphrates

Tigris

IRAQ
British Mandate

Mount Ararat

Van

ARMENIA

Kars

Erzerum

GEORGIA

C A U C A S U S

TRANS-JORDAN

Batum

Trabzon

SYRIA
French Mandate

RUSSIA

Odessa

Sebastopol

Danube

RUMANIA

Constanza

Burgas

BULGARIA

Sinope

Constantinople

B l a c k   S e a

Ankara

T U R K E Y

PALESTINE
British Mandate

Cairo

Nile

CYPRUS
British

Mediterranean   Sea

EGYPT
British Protectorate

Aegean Sea

Athens

G R E E C E

Proposed U.S. mandates

British proposal for a
further U.S. mandate

French control

British control

75

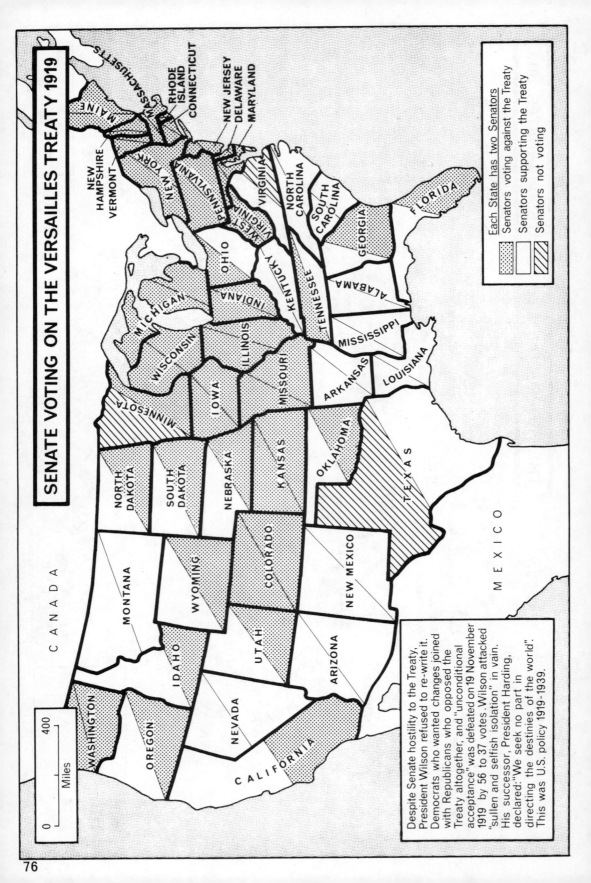

SENATE VOTING ON THE VERSAILLES TREATY 1919

Each State has two Senators

Senators voting against the Treaty

Senators supporting the Treaty

Senators not voting

Despite Senate hostility to the Treaty, President Wilson refused to re-write it. Democrats who wanted changes joined with Republicans who opposed the Treaty altogether, and "unconditional acceptance" was defeated on 19 November 1919 by 56 to 37 votes. Wilson attacked "sullen and selfish isolation" in vain. His successor, President Harding, declared: "We seek no part in directing the destinies of the world". This was U.S. policy 1919-1939.

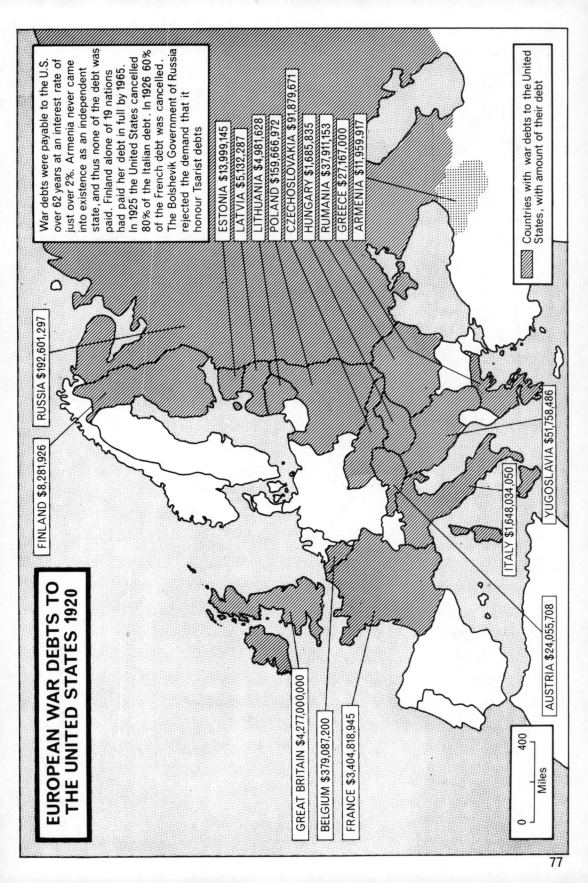

EUROPEAN WAR DEBTS TO THE UNITED STATES 1920

War debts were payable to the U.S. over 62 years at an interest rate of just over 2%. Armenia never came into existence as an independent state, and thus none of the debt was paid. Finland alone of 19 nations had paid her debt in full by 1965. In 1925 the United States cancelled 80% of the Italian debt. In 1926 60% of the French debt was cancelled. The Bolshevik Government of Russia rejected the demand that it honour Tsarist debts

ESTONIA $13,999,145
LATVIA $5,132,287
LITHUANIA $4,981,628
POLAND $159,666,972
CZECHOSLOVAKIA $91,879,671
HUNGARY $1,685,835
RUMANIA $37,911,153
GREECE $27,167,000
ARMENIA $11,959,917

RUSSIA $192,601,297

FINLAND $8,281,926

ITALY $1,648,034,050

YUGOSLAVIA $51,758,486

AUSTRIA $24,055,708

GREAT BRITAIN $4,277,000,000

BELGIUM $379,087,200

FRANCE $3,404,818,945

Countries with war debts to the United States, with amount of their debt

0   400
Miles

77

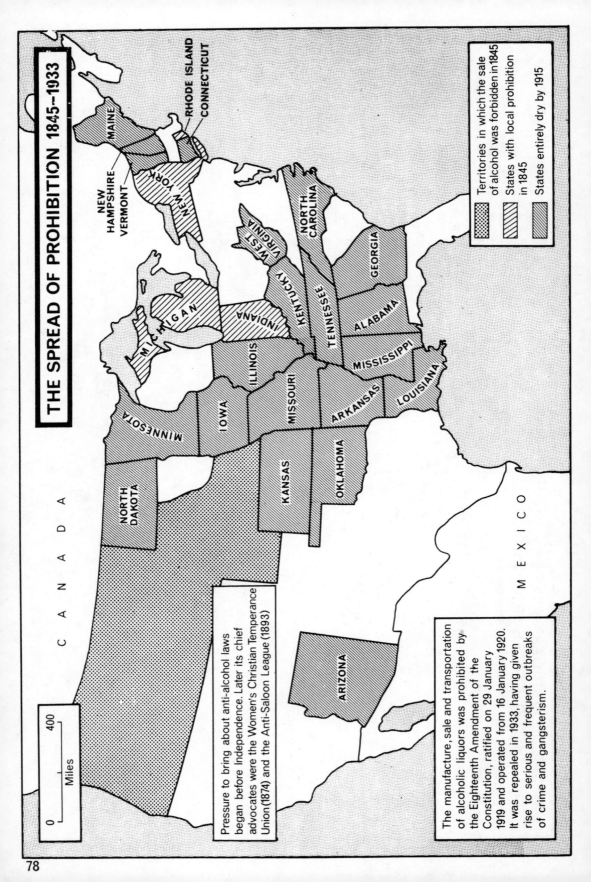

THE SPREAD OF PROHIBITION 1845—1933

Territories in which the sale of alcohol was forbidden in 1845

States with local prohibition in 1845

States entirely dry by 1915

CANADA

MEXICO

NORTH DAKOTA

MINNESOTA

MICHIGAN

NEW HAMPSHIRE
VERMONT

MAINE

RHODE ISLAND
CONNECTICUT

NEW YORK

WEST VIRGINIA

KENTUCKY

INDIANA

ILLINOIS

IOWA

MISSOURI

KANSAS

OKLAHOMA

ARKANSAS

LOUISIANA

MISSISSIPPI

ALABAMA

TENNESSEE

GEORGIA

NORTH CAROLINA

ARIZONA

0   400
Miles

Pressure to bring about anti-alcohol laws began before Independence. Later its chief advocates were the Women's Christian Temperance Union (1874) and the Anti-Saloon League (1893)

The manufacture, sale and transportation of alcoholic liquors was prohibited by the Eighteenth Amendment of the Constitution, ratified on 29 January 1919 and operated from 16 January 1920. It was repealed in 1933, having given rise to serious and frequent outbreaks of crime and gangsterism.

78

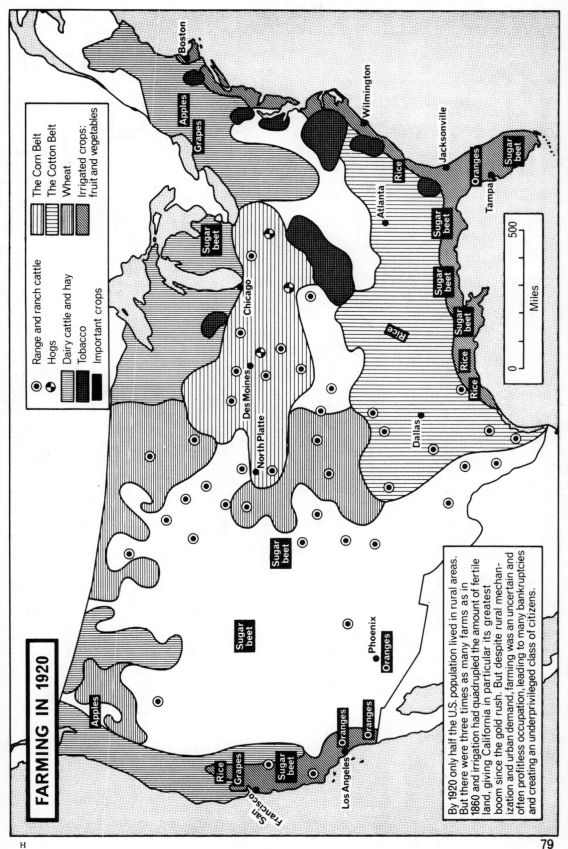

FARMING IN 1920

Legend:
- ⊙ Range and ranch cattle
- ✦ Hogs
- Dairy cattle and hay
- Tobacco
- Important crops

- The Corn Belt
- The Cotton Belt
- Wheat.
- Irrigated crops: fruit and vegetables

Boston

Apples

Grapes

Wilmington

Jacksonville

Rice

Sugar beet

Oranges

Atlanta

Tampa

Sugar beet

Sugar beet

Sugar beet

Rice

Chicago

Des Moines

Rice

Rice

North Platte

Rice

Dallas

Sugar beet

Sugar beet

Sugar beet

Phoenix

Oranges

Apples

Rice

Grapes

Sugar beet

Oranges

Oranges

Los Angeles

San Francisco

0   500
Miles

By 1920 only half the U.S. population lived in rural areas. But there were three times as many farms as in 1860 and irrigation had quadrupled the amount of fertile land, giving California in particular its greatest boom since the gold rush. But despite rural mechanization and urban demand, farming was an uncertain and often profitless occupation, leading to many bankruptcies and creating an underprivileged class of citizens.

H

79

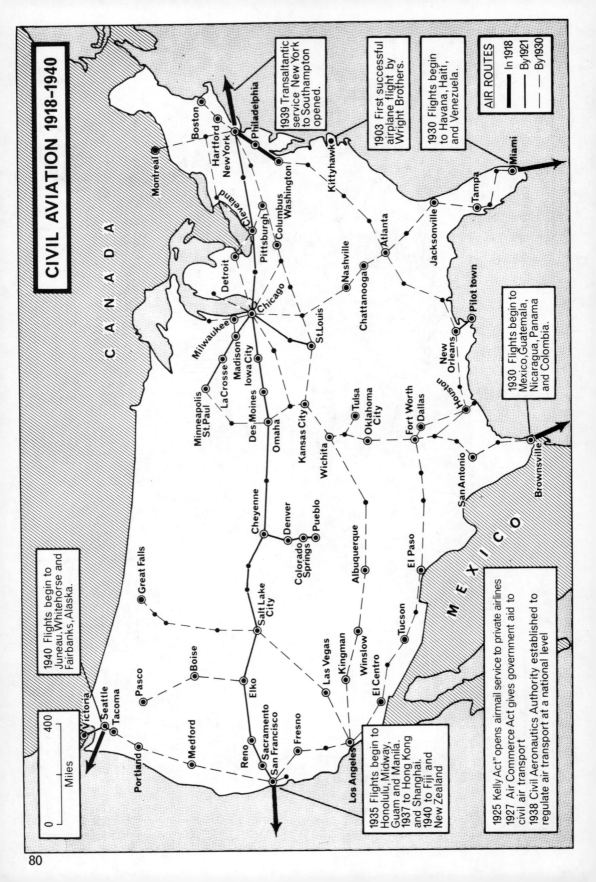

CIVIL AVIATION 1918–1940

CANADA

MEXICO

AIR ROUTES
In 1918
By 1921
By 1930

1939 Transatlantic service New York to Southampton opened.

1903 First successful airplane flight by Wright Brothers.

1930 Flights begin to Havana, Haiti, and Venezuela.

1930 Flights begin to Mexico, Guatemala, Nicaragua, Panama and Colombia.

1940 Flights begin to Juneau, Whitehorse and Fairbanks, Alaska.

1935 Flights begin to Honolulu, Midway, Guam and Manila. 1937 to Hong Kong and Shanghai. 1940 to Fiji and New Zealand.

1925 Kelly Act" opens airmail service to private airlines
1927 Air Commerce Act gives government aid to civil air transport
1938 Civil Aeronautics Authority established to regulate air transport at a national level

Miles
0   400

Boston
Hartford
New York
Philadelphia
Montreal
Cleveland
Columbus
Washington
Pittsburgh
Kittyhawk
Detroit
Nashville
Atlanta
Jacksonville
Chicago
St.Louis
Chattanooga
Tampa
Miami
Pilot town
New Orleans
Houston
Milwaukee
Madison
Iowa City
Minneapolis St.Paul
La Crosse
Des Moines
Omaha
Kansas City
Wichita
Tulsa
Oklahoma City
Fort Worth
Dallas
San Antonio
Brownsville
Cheyenne
Denver
Pueblo
Colorado Springs
Albuquerque
El Paso
Tucson
Great Falls
Salt Lake City
Las Vegas
Kingman
Winslow
El Centro
Victoria
Seattle
Tacoma
Portland
Pasco
Boise
Medford
Elko
Reno
Sacramento
San Francisco
Fresno
Los Angeles

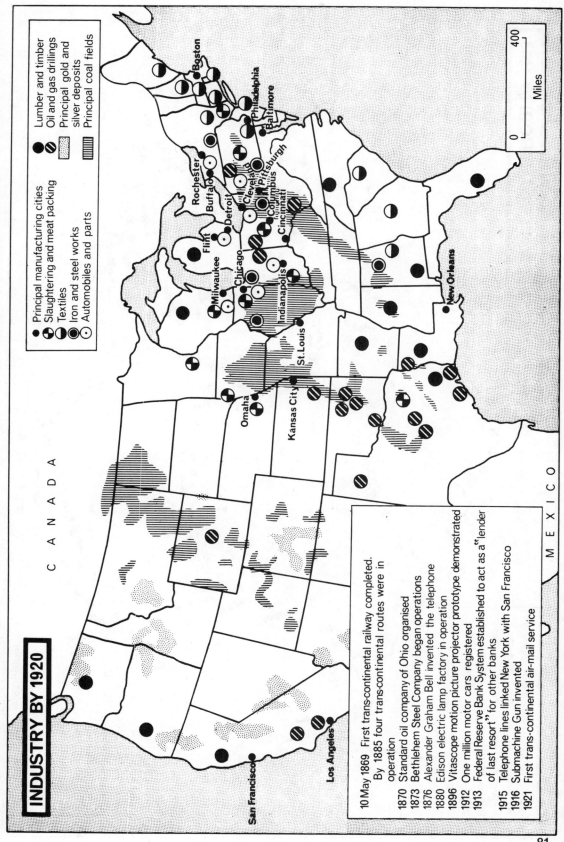

INDUSTRY BY 1920

Legend:

Principal manufacturing cities •
Slaughtering and meat packing ⊕
Textiles ◐
Iron and steel works ◉
Automobiles and parts ⊙

Lumber and timber ●
Oil and gas drillings ⦸
Principal gold and silver deposits ▦
Principal coal fields ▥

C A N A D A

M E X I C O

Boston
Philadelphia
Baltimore
Pittsburgh
Rochester
Buffalo
Cleveland
Columbus
Detroit
Cincinnati
Flint
Milwaukee
Chicago
Indianapolis
St. Louis
Omaha
Kansas City
New Orleans
San Francisco
Los Angeles

400
0
Miles

10 May 1869 First trans-continental railway completed.
By 1885 four trans-continental routes were in operation

1870 Standard oil company of Ohio organised
1873 Bethlehem Steel Company began operations
1876 Alexander Graham Bell invented the telephone
1880 Edison electric lamp factory in operation
1896 Vitascope motion picture projector prototype demonstrated
1912 One million motor cars registered
1913 Federal Reserve Bank System established to act as a "lender of last resort" for other banks
1915 Telephone lines linked New York with San Francisco
1916 Submachine Gun invented
1921 First trans-continental air-mail service

81

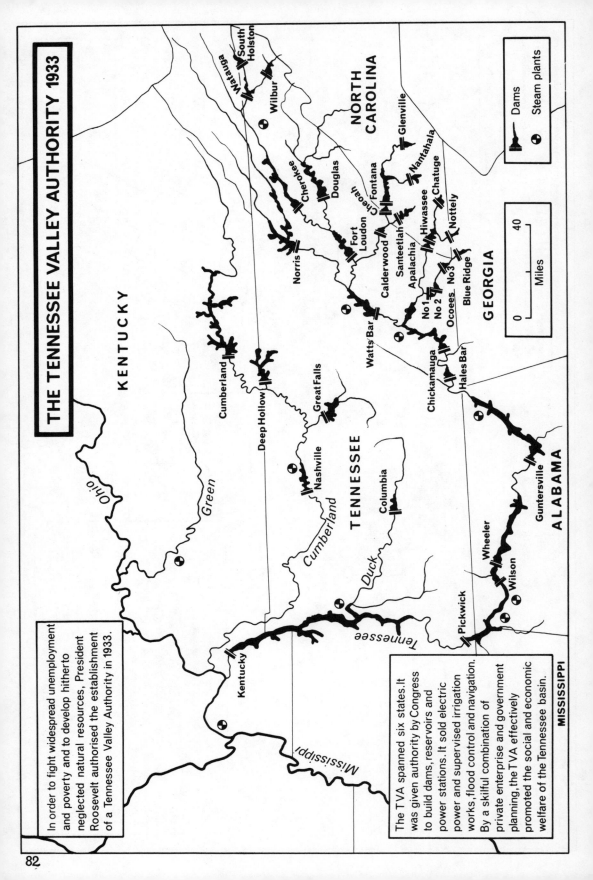

THE TENNESSEE VALLEY AUTHORITY 1933

In order to fight widespread unemployment and poverty and to develop hitherto neglected natural resources, President Roosevelt authorised the establishment of a Tennessee Valley Authority in 1933.

The TVA spanned six states. It was given authority by Congress to build dams, reservoirs and power stations. It sold electric power and supervised irrigation works, flood control and navigation. By a skilful combination of private enterprise and government planning, the TVA effectively promoted the social and economic welfare of the Tennessee basin.

Dams

Steam plants

0   40

Miles

KENTUCKY

TENNESSEE

NORTH CAROLINA

GEORGIA

ALABAMA

MISSISSIPPI

Ohio

Green

Cumberland

Duck

Tennessee

Mississippi

South Holston

Watauga

Wilbur

Cherokee

Douglas

Glenville

Nantahala

Cheoah

Fontana

Chatuge

Fort Loudon

Hiwassee

Nottely

Calderwood

Santeetlah

Apalachia

No 1

No 2

Ocoees No3

Blue Ridge

Norris

Watts Bar

Chickamauga

Hales Bar

Cumberland

Deep Hollow

Great Falls

Nashville

Columbia

Kentucky

Pickwick

Wheeler

Wilson

Guntersville

82

THE UNITED STATES 1914–1945

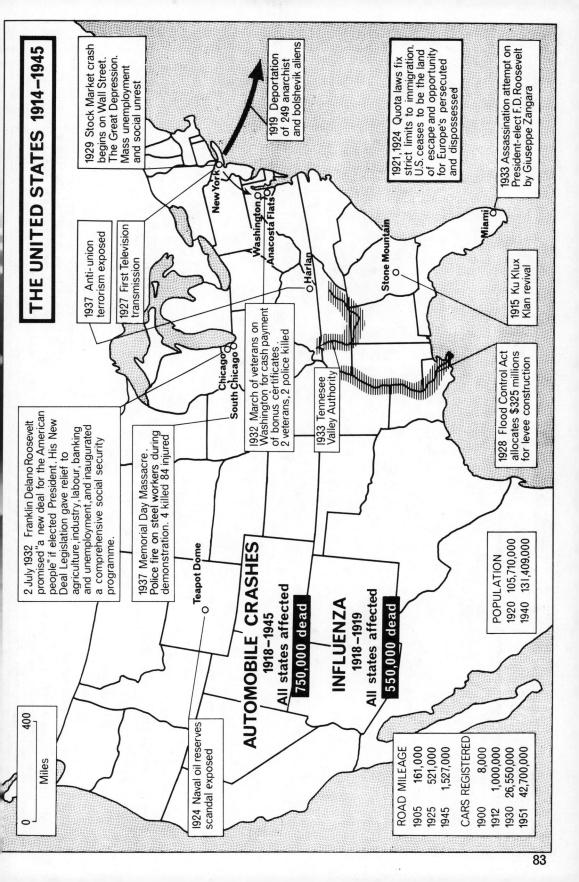

1929 Stock Market crash begins on Wall Street. The Great Depression. Mass unemployment and social unrest

1919 Deportation of 249 anarchist and bolshevik aliens

1921, 1924 Quota laws fix strict limits to immigration. U.S. ceases to be the land of escape and opportunity for Europe's persecuted and dispossessed

1933 Assassination attempt on President-elect F.D. Roosevelt by Giuseppe Zangara

1937 Anti-union terrorism exposed

1927 First Television transmission

New York

Washington
Anacosta Flats

Harlan

Stone Mountain

Miami

1915 Ku Klux Klan revival

Chicago
South Chicago

1932 March of veterans on Washington for cash payment of bonus certificates 2 veterans, 2 police killed

1933 Tennessee Valley Authority

1928 Flood Control Act allocates $325 millions for levee construction

2 July 1932 Franklin Delano Roosevelt promised "a new deal for the American people" if elected President. His New Deal Legislation gave relief to agriculture, industry, labour, banking and unemployment, and inaugurated a comprehensive social security programme.

1937 Memorial Day Massacre. Police fire on steel workers during demonstration. 4 killed 84 injured

Teapot Dome

AUTOMOBILE CRASHES
1918–1945
All states affected
750,000 dead

INFLUENZA
1918–1919
All states affected
550,000 dead

1924 Naval oil reserves scandal exposed

0			400
	Miles		

POPULATION	
1920	105,710,000
1940	131,409,000

ROAD MILEAGE	
1905	161,000
1925	521,000
1945	1,527,000

CARS REGISTERED	
1900	8,000
1912	1,000,000
1930	26,550,000
1951	42,700,000

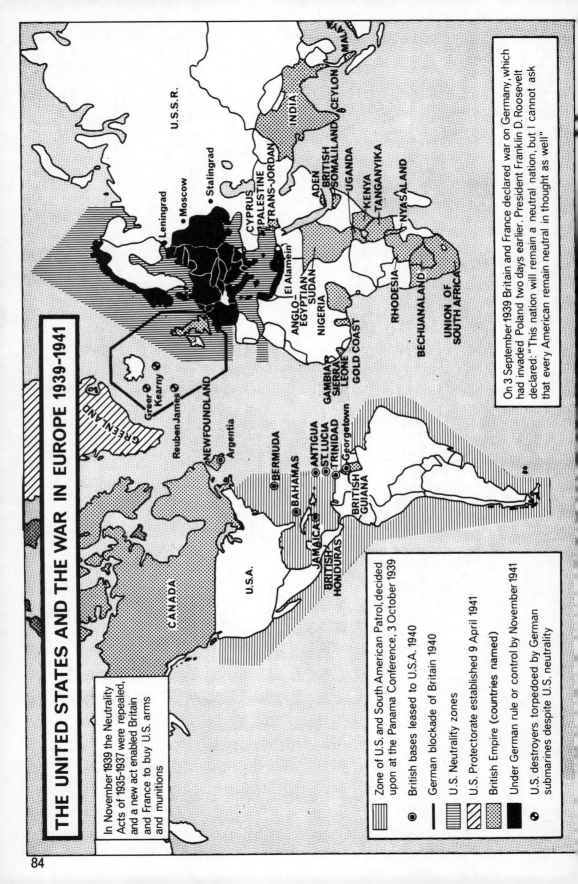

THE UNITED STATES AND THE WAR IN EUROPE 1939-1941

In November 1939 the Neutrality Acts of 1935-1937 were repealed, and a new act enabled Britain and France to buy U.S. arms and munitions

On 3 September 1939 Britain and France declared war on Germany, which had invaded Poland two days earlier. President Franklin D. Roosevelt declared: "This nation will remain a neutral nation, but I cannot ask that every American remain neutral in thought as well"

Zone of U.S. and South American Patrol, decided upon at the Panama Conference, 3 October 1939

British bases leased to U.S.A. 1940

German blockade of Britain 1940

U.S. Neutrality zones

U.S. Protectorate established 9 April 1941

British Empire (countries named)

Under German rule or control by November 1941

U.S. destroyers torpedoed by German submarines despite U.S. neutrality

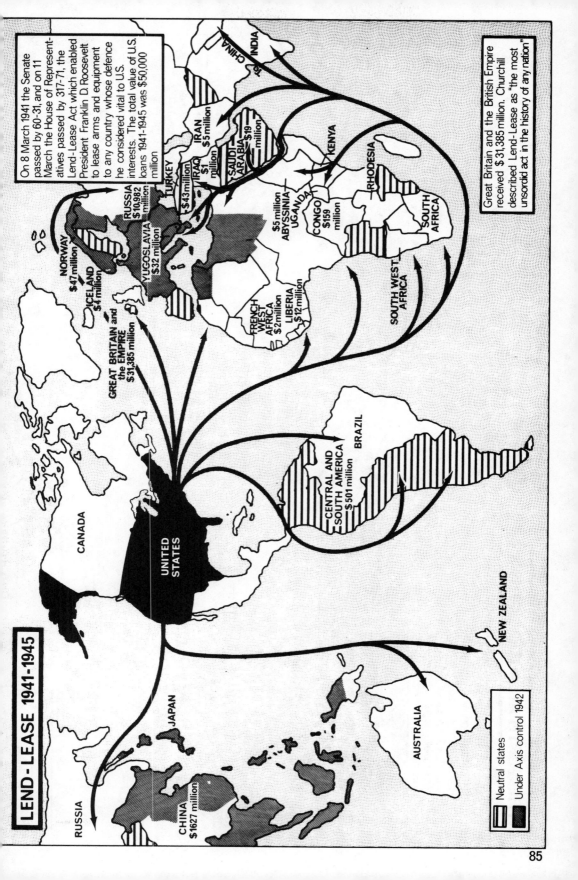

LEND-LEASE 1941-1945

On 8 March 1941 the Senate passed by 60-31, and on 11 March the House of Representatives passed by 317-71, the Lend-Lease Act which enabled President Franklin D. Roosevelt to lease arms and equipment to any country whose defence he considered vital to U.S. interests. The total value of U.S. loans 1941-1945 was $50,000 million

Great Britain and the British Empire received $ 31,385 million. Churchill described Lend-Lease as "the most unsordid act in the history of any nation"

RUSSIA
$10,982 million

NORWAY
$47 million

ICELAND
$4 million

GREAT BRITAIN and the EMPIRE
$31,385 million

YUGOSLAVIA
$32 million

TURKEY
$43million

IRAQ
$1 million

IRAN
$5 million

SAUDI-ARABIA $19 million

INDIA

CHINA

KENYA

RHODESIA

SOUTH AFRICA

CONGO
$159 million

UGANDA

ABYSSINIA
$5 million

SOUTH WEST AFRICA

LIBERIA
$12million

FRENCH WEST AFRICA
$2 million

CANADA

UNITED STATES

BRAZIL

CENTRAL AND SOUTH AMERICA
$ 501 million

NEW ZEALAND

RUSSIA

JAPAN

CHINA
$1627 million

AUSTRALIA

Neutral states

Under Axis control 1942

85

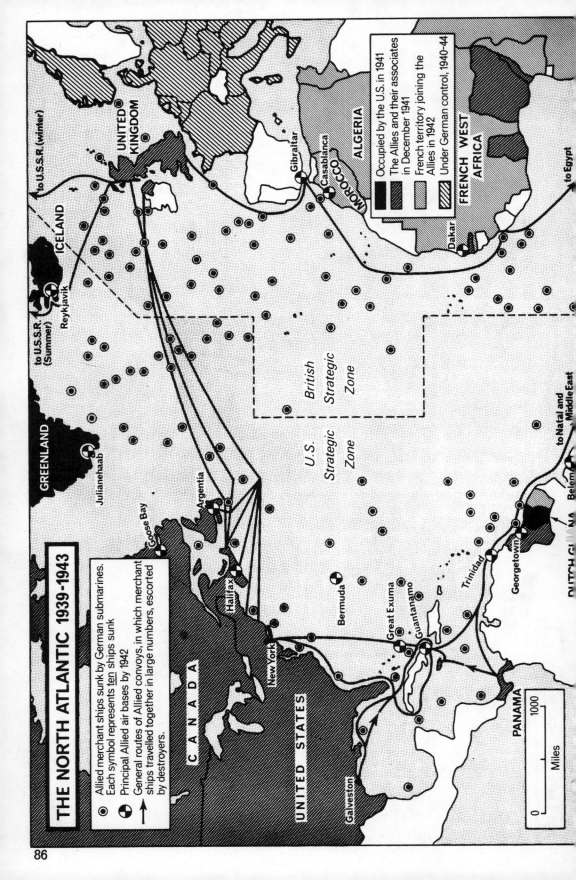

THE NORTH ATLANTIC 1939-1943

- ◉ Allied merchant ships sunk by German submarines. Each symbol represents ten ships sunk
- ☣ Principal Allied air bases by 1942
- ↑ General routes of Allied convoys, in which merchant ships travelled together in large numbers, escorted by destroyers.

GREENLAND

Julianehaab

ICELAND

Reykjavik

to U.S.S.R. (Summer)

to U.S.S.R. (winter)

UNITED KINGDOM

CANADA

Goose Bay

Argentia

Halifax

New York

Galveston

UNITED STATES

Bermuda

Great Exuma

Guantanamo

Trinidad

Georgetown

DUTCH GUIANA

Belem

PANAMA

to Natal and Middle East

U.S. Strategic Zone

British Strategic Zone

Gibraltar

Casablanca

MOROCCO

ALGERIA

Dakar

FRENCH WEST AFRICA

to Egypt

Occupied by the U.S. in 1941

The Allies and their associates in December 1941

French territory joining the Allies in 1942

Under German control, 1940-44

Miles

0   1000

86

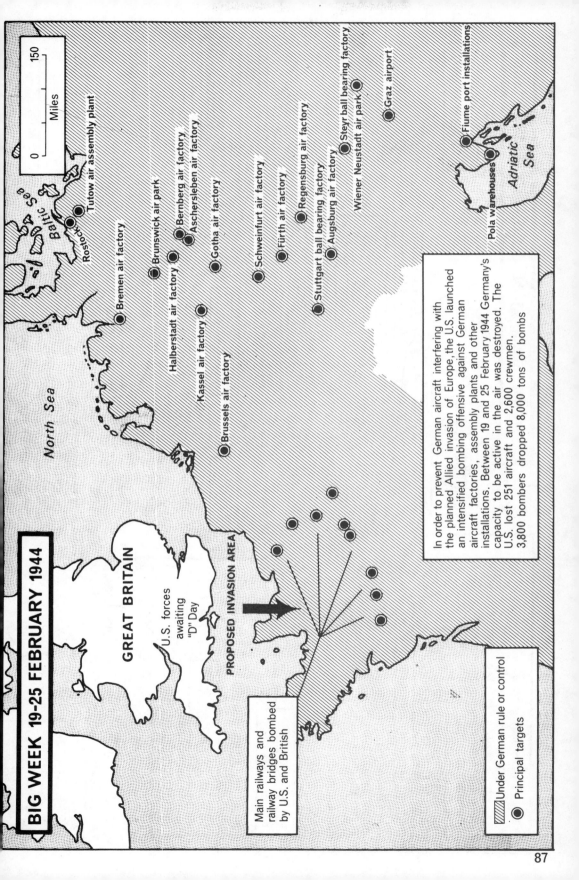

BIG WEEK 19-25 FEBRUARY 1944

GREAT BRITAIN

U.S. forces awaiting "D" Day

PROPOSED INVASION AREA

North Sea

Baltic Sea

Adriatic Sea

Tutow air assembly plant

Rostock

Bremen air factory

Brunswick air park

Halberstadt air factory

Bernberg air factory

Aschersleben air factory

Gotha air factory

Kassel air factory

Brussels air factory

Schweinfurt air factory

Fürth air factory

Regensburg air factory

Stuttgart ball bearing factory

Augsburg air factory

Steyr ball bearing factory

Wiener Neustadt air park

Graz airport

Fiume port installations

Pola warehouses

0 — 150 Miles

In order to prevent German aircraft interfering with the planned Allied invasion of Europe, the U.S. launched an intensified bombing offensive against German aircraft factories, assembly plants and other installations. Between 19 and 25 February 1944 Germany's capacity to be active in the air was destroyed. The U.S. lost 251 aircraft and 2,600 crewmen. 3,800 bombers dropped 8,000 tons of bombs

Main railways and railway bridges bombed by U.S. and British

Under German rule or control

Principal targets

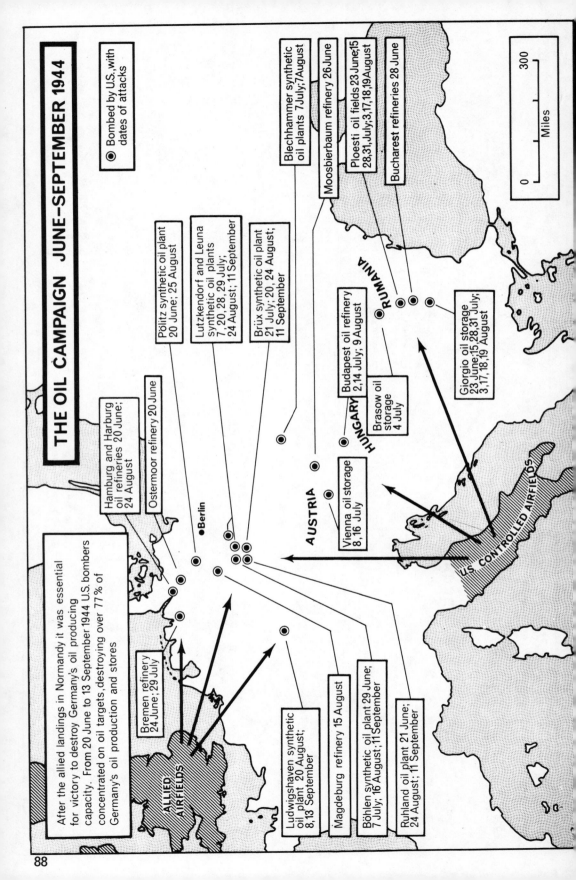

THE OIL CAMPAIGN JUNE–SEPTEMBER 1944

⊙ Bombed by U.S., with dates of attacks

After the allied landings in Normandy it was essential for victory to destroy Germany's oil producing capacity. From 20 June to 13 September 1944 U.S. bombers concentrated on oil targets, destroying over 77% of Germany's oil production and stores

Hamburg and Harburg oil refineries 20 June; 24 August

Ostermoor refinery 20 June

Pölitz synthetic oil plant 20 June; 25 August

Lutzkendorf and Leuna synthetic oil plants 7, 20, 28, 29 July; 24 August; 11 September

Brüx synthetic oil plant 21 July; 20, 24 August; 11 September

Blechhammer synthetic oil plants 7 July; 7 August

Moosbierbaum refinery 26 June

Ploesti oil fields 23 June;15 28,31,July;3,17,18,19August

Bucharest refineries 28 June

Giorgio oil storage 23 June;15,28,31 July; 3,17,18,19 August

Budapest oil refinery 2,14 July; 9 August

Brasow oil storage 4 July

Vienna oil storage 8, 16 July

Bremen refinery 24 June; 29 July

Ludwigshaven synthetic oil plant 20 August; 8,13 September

Magdeburg refinery 15 August

Böhlen synthetic oil plant 29 June; 7 July; 16 August;11September

Ruhland oil plant 21 June; 24 August; 11 September

●Berlin

AUSTRIA

HUNGARY

RUMANIA

U.S. CONTROLLED AIRFIELDS

ALLIED AIRFIELDS

0   300

Miles

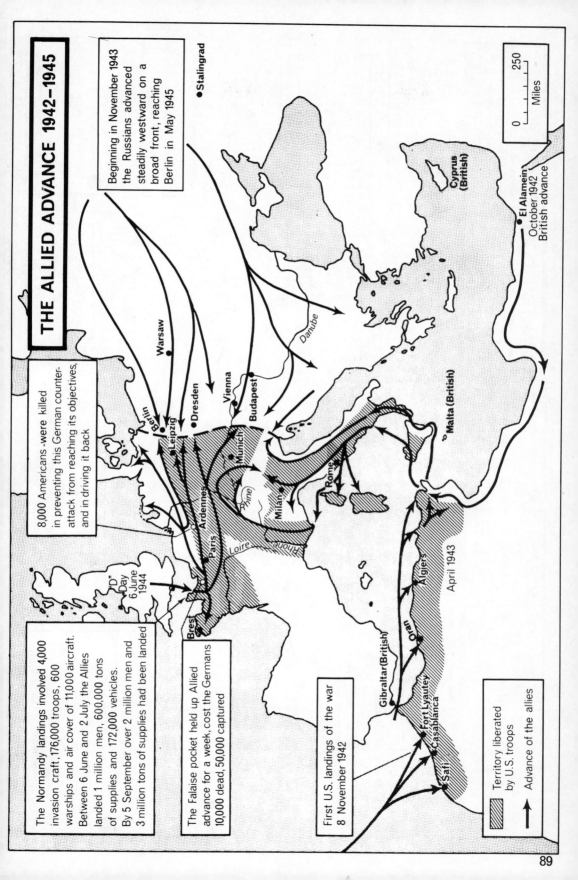

THE ALLIED ADVANCE 1942-1945

Beginning in November 1943 the Russians advanced steadily westward on a broad front, reaching Berlin in May 1945

8,000 Americans were killed in preventing this German counter-attack from reaching its objectives, and in driving it back

The Normandy landings involved 4,000 invasion craft, 176,000 troops, 600 warships and air cover of 11,000 aircraft. Between 6 June and 2 July the Allies landed 1 million men, 600,000 tons of supplies and 172,000 vehicles. By 5 September over 2 million men and 3 million tons of supplies had been landed

The Falaise pocket held up Allied advance for a week, cost the Germans 10,000 dead, 50,000 captured

First U.S. landings of the war 8 November 1942

El Alamein
October 1942
British advance

"D" Day 6 June 1944

Territory liberated by U.S. troops

Advance of the allies

Stalingrad

Warsaw

Berlin
Leipzig
Dresden
Vienna
Budapest
Munich
Danube

Paris
Loire
Ardennes
Rhine
Rhône
Milan
Rome

Brest

Gibraltar(British)
Oran
Algiers
Fort Lyautey
Casablanca
Safi

April 1943

Malta (British)

Cyprus (British)

0   250
Miles

89

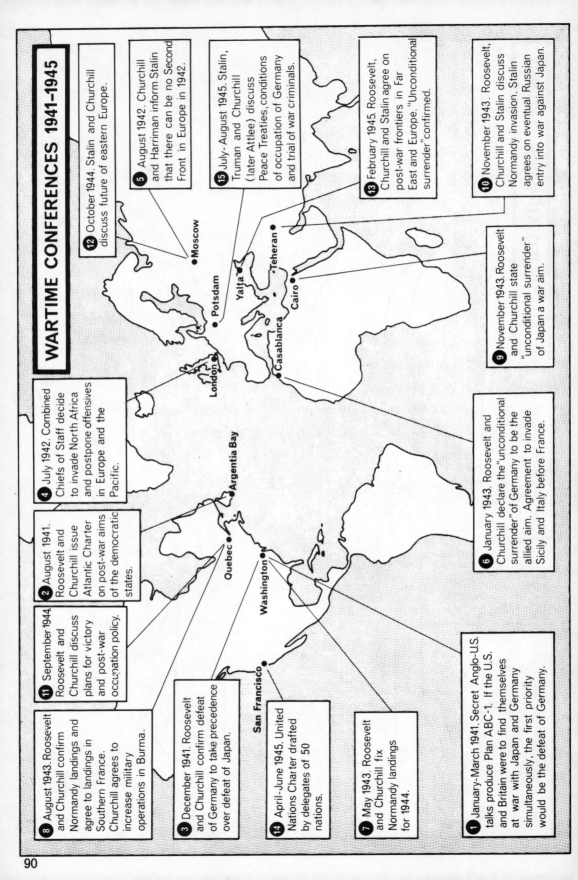

WARTIME CONFERENCES 1941–1945

12 October 1944. Stalin and Churchill discuss future of eastern Europe.

5 August 1942. Churchill and Harriman inform Stalin that there can be no Second Front in Europe in 1942.

15 July–August 1945. Stalin, Truman and Churchill (later Attlee) discuss Peace Treaties, conditions of occupation of Germany and trial of war criminals.

13 February 1945. Roosevelt, Churchill and Stalin agree on post-war frontiers in Far East and Europe. "Unconditional surrender" confirmed.

10 November 1943. Roosevelt, Churchill and Stalin discuss Normandy invasion. Stalin agrees on eventual Russian entry into war against Japan.

9 November 1943. Roosevelt and Churchill state "unconditional surrender" of Japan a war aim.

4 July 1942. Combined Chiefs of Staff decide to invade North Africa and postpone offensives in Europe and the Pacific.

2 August 1941. Roosevelt and Churchill issue Atlantic Charter on post-war aims of the democratic states.

11 September 1944. Roosevelt and Churchill discuss plans for victory and post-war occupation policy.

6 January 1943. Roosevelt and Churchill declare the "unconditional surrender" of Germany to be the allied aim. Agreement to invade Sicily and Italy before France.

8 August 1943. Roosevelt and Churchill confirm Normandy landings and agree to landings in Southern France. Churchill agrees to increase military operations in Burma.

3 December 1941. Roosevelt and Churchill confirm defeat of Germany to take precedence over defeat of Japan.

14 April–June 1945. United Nations Charter drafted by delegates of 50 nations.

7 May 1943. Roosevelt and Churchill fix Normandy landings for 1944.

1 January–March 1941. Secret Anglo-U.S. talks produce Plan ABC-1. If the U.S. and Britain were to find themselves at war with Japan and Germany simultaneously, the first priority would be the defeat of Germany.

Moscow
Potsdam
Yalta
Teheran
Casablanca
Cairo
London
Argentia Bay
Quebec
Washington
San Francisco

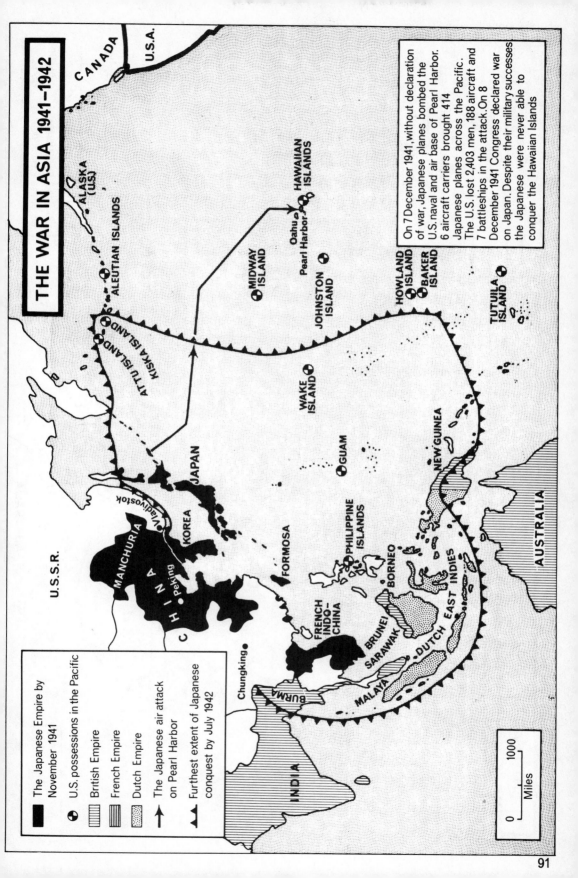

THE WAR IN ASIA 1941–1942

On 7 December 1941, without declaration of war, Japanese planes bombed the U.S. naval and air base of Pearl Harbor. 6 aircraft carriers brought 414 Japanese planes across the Pacific. The U.S. lost 2,403 men, 188 aircraft and 7 battleships in the attack. On 8 December 1941 Congress declared war on Japan. Despite their military successes the Japanese were never able to conquer the Hawaiian Islands

U.S.S.R.

CANADA

U.S.A.

ALASKA (U.S.)

ALEUTIAN ISLANDS

ATTU ISLAND

KISKA ISLAND

MIDWAY ISLAND

HAWAIIAN ISLANDS

Oahu

Pearl Harbor

JOHNSTON ISLAND

WAKE ISLAND

HOWLAND ISLAND

BAKER ISLAND

TUTUILA ISLAND

Vladivostok

JAPAN

KOREA

MANCHURIA

C H I N A

Peking

FORMOSA

GUAM

PHILIPPINE ISLANDS

NEW GUINEA

AUSTRALIA

FRENCH INDO-CHINA

BORNEO

BRUNEI

SARAWAK

DUTCH EAST INDIES

MALAYA

BURMA

Chungking

INDIA

Legend:
- The Japanese Empire by November 1941
- U.S. possessions in the Pacific
- British Empire
- French Empire
- Dutch Empire
- The Japanese air attack on Pearl Harbor
- Furthest extent of Japanese conquest by July 1942

0   1000
Miles

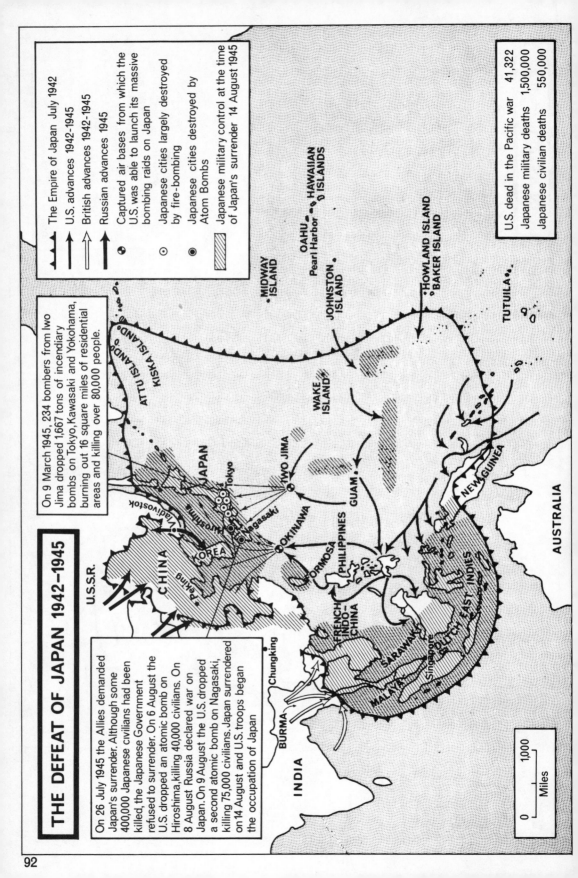

THE DEFEAT OF JAPAN 1942–1945

On 9 March 1945, 234 bombers from Iwo Jima dropped 1,667 tons of incendiary bombs on Tokyo, Kawasaki and Yokohama, burning out 16 square miles of residential areas and killing over 80,000 people.

On 26 July 1945 the Allies demanded Japan's surrender. Although some 400,000 Japanese civilians had been killed, the Japanese Government refused to surrender. On 6 August the U.S. dropped an atomic bomb on Hiroshima, killing 40,000 civilians. On 8 August Russia declared war on Japan. On 9 August the U.S. dropped a second atomic bomb on Nagasaki, killing 75,000 civilians. Japan surrendered on 14 August and U.S. troops began the occupation of Japan

Legend

- The Empire of Japan July 1942
- U.S. advances 1942-1945
- British advances 1942-1945
- Russian advances 1945
- Captured air bases from which the U.S. was able to launch its massive bombing raids on Japan
- Japanese cities largely destroyed by fire-bombing
- Japanese cities destroyed by Atom Bombs
- Japanese military control at the time of Japan's surrender 14 August 1945

U.S. dead in the Pacific war	41,322
Japanese military deaths	1,500,000
Japanese civilian deaths	550,000

U.S.S.R.

CHINA

Vladivostok

Peking

Chungking

INDIA

BURMA

KOREA

JAPAN

Tokyo

Hiroshima

Nagasaki

OKINAWA

FORMOSA

PHILIPPINES

FRENCH INDO-CHINA

MALAYA

Singapore

SARAWAK

DUTCH EAST INDIES

NEW GUINEA

AUSTRALIA

ATTU ISLAND

KISKA ISLAND

IWO JIMA

GUAM

WAKE ISLAND

MIDWAY ISLAND

JOHNSTON ISLAND

OAHU

Pearl Harbor

HAWAIIAN ISLANDS

HOWLAND ISLAND

BAKER ISLAND

TUTUILA

0   1,000

Miles

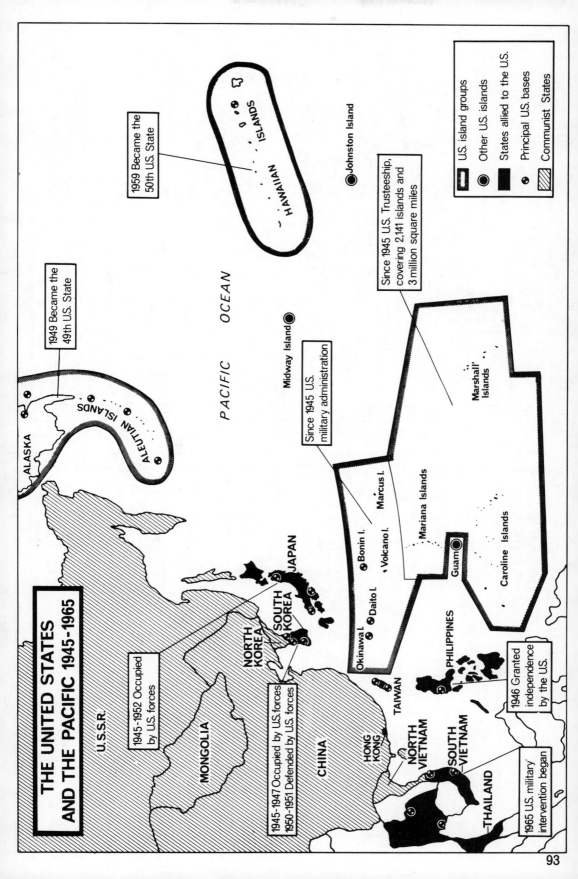

THE UNITED STATES AND THE PACIFIC 1945-1965

U.S.S.R.

MONGOLIA

CHINA

ALASKA

1949 Became the 49th U.S. State

ALEUTIAN ISLANDS

PACIFIC OCEAN

Midway Island

1959 Became the 50th U.S. State

HAWAIIAN ISLANDS

Johnston Island

Since 1945 U.S. Trusteeship, covering 2,141 islands and 3 million square miles

Since 1945 U.S. military administration

Marshall Islands

Bonin I.

Volcano I.

Marcus I.

Mariana Islands

Caroline Islands

Guam

Okinawa I.

Daito I.

JAPAN

SOUTH KOREA

NORTH KOREA

1945-1952 Occupied by U.S. forces

1945-1947 Occupied by U.S. forces
1950-1951 Defended by U.S. forces

HONG KONG

TAIWAN

PHILIPPINES

1946 Granted independence by the U.S.

NORTH VIETNAM

SOUTH VIETNAM

THAILAND

1965 U.S. military intervention began

U.S. island groups
Other U.S. islands
States allied to the U.S.
Principal U.S. bases
Communist States

93

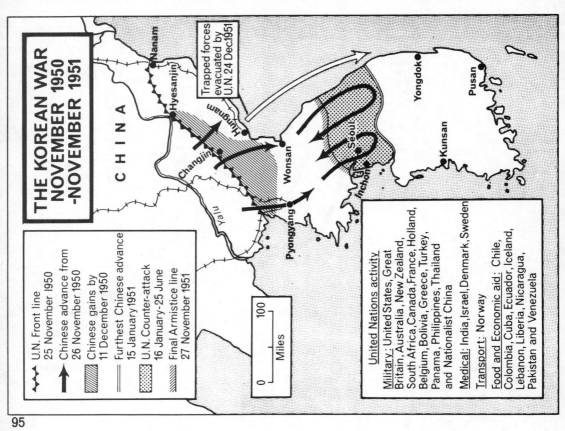

THE KOREAN WAR NOVEMBER 1950 -NOVEMBER 1951

Trapped forces evacuated by U.N. 24 Dec 1951

C H I N A

Nanam
Hyesanjin
Hungnam
Changjin
Yalu
Wonsan
Seoul
Inchon
Pyongyang

Yongdok
Pusan
Kunsan

Legend

⋀⋀⋀	U.N. Front line 25 November 1950
↑	Chinese advance from 26 November 1950
▨	Chinese gains by 11 December 1950
═══	Furthest Chinese advance 15 January 1951
▦	U.N. Counter-attack 16 January-25 June
▥	Final Armistice line 27 November 1951

0 ———— 100
Miles

United Nations activity

<u>Military</u>: United States, Great Britain, Australia, New Zealand, South Africa, Canada, France, Holland, Belgium, Bolivia, Greece, Turkey, Panama, Philippines, Thailand and Nationalist China

<u>Medical</u>: India, Israel, Denmark, Sweden

<u>Transport</u>: Norway

<u>Food and Economic aid</u>: Chile, Colombia, Cuba, Ecuador, Iceland, Lebanon, Liberia, Nicaragua, Pakistan and Venezuela

95

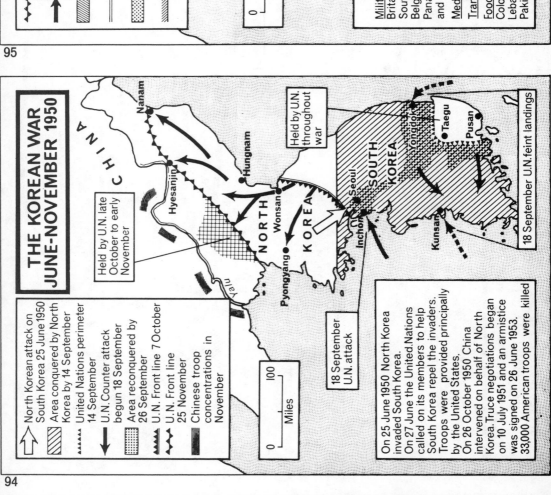

THE KOREAN WAR JUNE-NOVEMBER 1950

Nanam

C H I N A

Held by U.N. late October to early November

Hyesanjin
Hungnam
Yalu
Wonsan
NORTH
KOREA
Pyongyang

Held by U.N. throughout war

Seoul
Inchon
SOUTH
KOREA
Kunsan

Yongdok
Taegu
Pusan

18 September U.N. feint landings

18 September U.N. attack

Legend

⇪	North Korean attack on South Korea 25 June 1950
▨	Area conquered by North Korea by 14 September
▴▴▴	United Nations perimeter 14 September
↓	U.N. Counter attack begun 18 September
▦	Area reconquered by 26 September
⋀⋀⋀	U.N. Front line 7 October
⋀⋀⋀	U.N. Front line 25 November
▰	Chinese troop concentrations in November

0 ———— 100
Miles

On 25 June 1950 North Korea invaded South Korea.
On 27 June the United Nations called on its members to help South Korea repel the invaders. Troops were provided principally by the United States.
On 26 October 1950 China intervened on behalf of North Korea. Truce negotiations began on 10 July 1951 and an armistice was signed on 26 June 1953. 33,000 American troops were killed

94

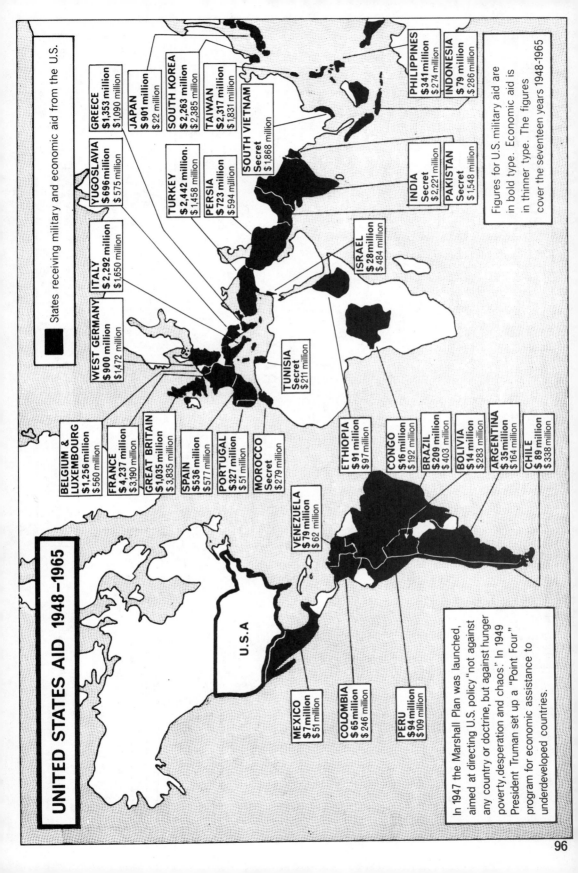

UNITED STATES AID 1948–1965

States receiving military and economic aid from the U.S.

Figures for U.S. military aid are in bold type. Economic aid is in thinner type. The figures cover the seventeen years 1948-1965.

In 1947 the Marshall Plan was launched, aimed at directing U.S. policy "not against any country or doctrine, but against hunger poverty, desperation and chaos". In 1949 President Truman set up a "Point Four" program for economic assistance to underdeveloped countries.

U.S.A

BELGIUM & LUXEMBOURG
$1,256 million
$ 560 million

FRANCE
$ 4,237 million
$ 3,190 million

GREAT BRITAIN
$ 1,035 million
$ 3,835 million

SPAIN
$ 536 million
$ 577 million

PORTUGAL
$ 327 million
$ 51 million

MOROCCO
Secret
$ 279 million

WEST GERMANY
$ 900 million
$ 1,472 million

ITALY
$ 2,292 million
$ 1,650 million

YUGOSLAVIA
$ 696 million
$ 575 million

GREECE
$ 1,353 million
$ 1,090 million

JAPAN
$ 901 million
$ 22 million

SOUTH KOREA
$ 2,263 million
$ 2,385 million

TAIWAN
$ 2,317 million
$ 1,831 million

SOUTH VIETNAM
Secret
$ 1,868 million

TURKEY
$ 2,442 million.
$ 1,458 million

PERSIA
$ 723 million
$ 594 million

ISRAEL
$ 28 million
$ 484 million

TUNISIA
Secret
$ 211 million

INDIA
Secret
$ 2,221 million

PAKISTAN
Secret
$ 1,548 million

PHILIPPINES
$ 341 million
$ 274 million

INDONESIA
$ 79 million
$ 286 million

VENEZUELA
$ 79 million
$ 62 million

MEXICO
$ 7 million
$ 51 million

COLOMBIA
$ 65 million
$ 246 million

PERU
$ 94 million
$ 109 million

ETHIOPIA
$ 91 million
$ 97 million

CONGO
$ 16 million
$ 192 million

BRAZIL
$ 209 million
$ 403 million

BOLIVIA
$ 14 million
$ 283 million

ARGENTINA
$ 35 million
$ 164 million

CHILE
$ 89 million
$ 338 million

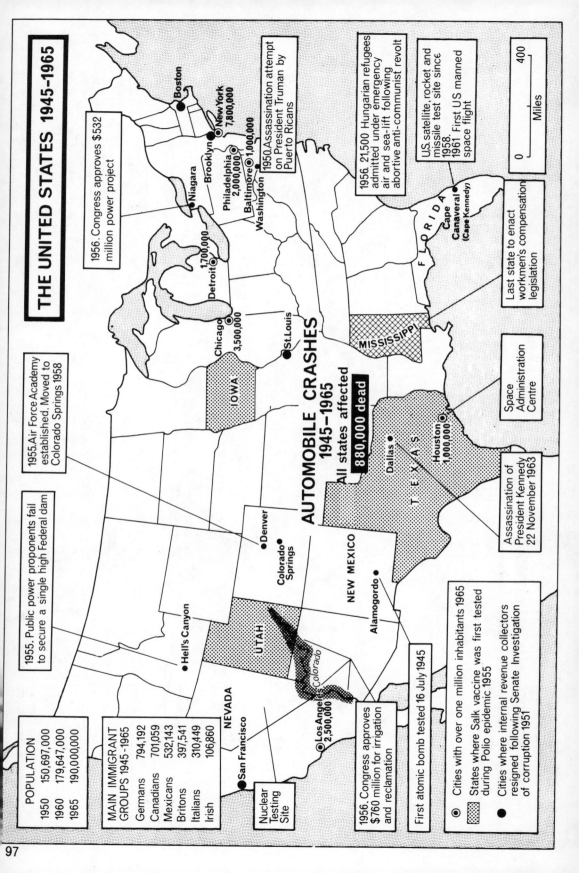

THE UNITED STATES 1945-1965

1956. Congress approves $532 million power project

1950. Assassination attempt on President Truman by Puerto Ricans

1956. 21,500 Hungarian refugees admitted under emergency air and sea-lift following abortive anti-communist revolt

U.S. satellite, rocket and missile test site since 1958. 1961 First US manned space flight

Last state to enact workmen's compensation legislation

Space Administration Centre

Assassination of President Kennedy 22 November 1963

1955. Air Force Academy established. Moved to Colorado Springs 1958

1955. Public power proponents fail to secure a single high Federal dam

POPULATION

1950	150,697,000
1960	179,647,000
1965	190,000,000

MAIN IMMIGRANT GROUPS 1945-1965

Germans	794,192
Canadians	701,059
Mexicans	532,143
Britons	397,541
Italians	310,449
Irish	106,860

Nuclear Testing Site

1956. Congress approves $760 million for irrigation and reclamation

First atomic bomb tested 16 July 1945

AUTOMOBILE CRASHES 1945-1965
All states affected
880,000 dead

Boston

New York 7,800,000

Brooklyn 2,000,000

Niagara

Philadelphia 1,000,000

Baltimore 1,000,000

Washington

Detroit 1,700,000

Chicago 3,500,000

St. Louis

MISSISSIPPI

FLORIDA

Cape Canaveral (Cape Kennedy)

IOWA

Dallas

Houston 1,000,000

T E X A S

Denver

Colorado Springs

NEW MEXICO

Alamogordo

Colorado

UTAH

Hell's Canyon

NEVADA

Los Angeles 2,500,000

San Francisco

⊙ Cities with over one million inhabitants 1965

States where Salk vaccine was first tested during Polio epidemic 1955

● Cities where internal revenue collectors resigned following Senate Investigation of corruption 1951

0		400

Miles

97

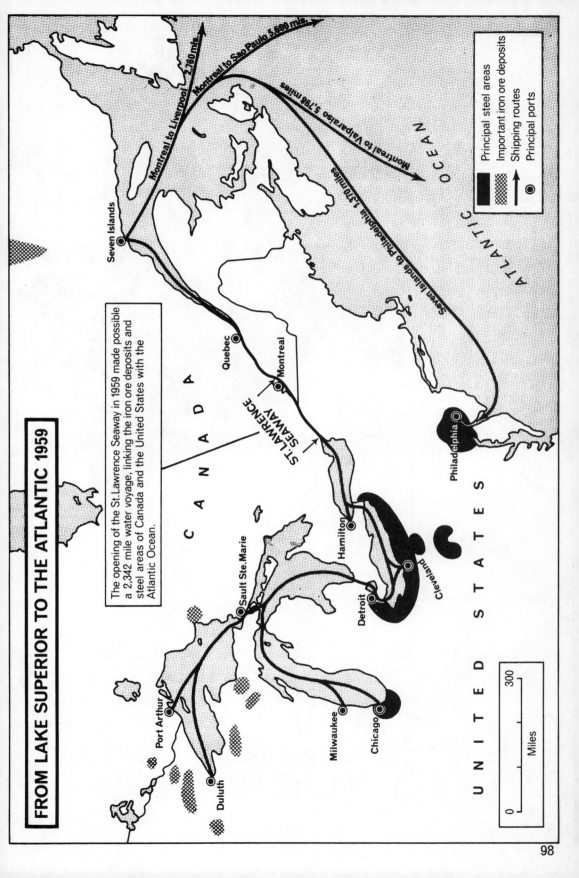

FROM LAKE SUPERIOR TO THE ATLANTIC 1959

The opening of the St. Lawrence Seaway in 1959 made possible a 2,342 mile water voyage, linking the iron ore deposits and steel areas of Canada and the United States with the Atlantic Ocean.

Montreal to Liverpool 3,760 mls.

Montreal to Sao Paulo 5,609 mls.

Montreal to Valparaiso 5,798 miles

Seven Islands to Philadelphia 1,370 miles

ATLANTIC OCEAN

ST. LAWRENCE SEAWAY

C A N A D A

U N I T E D   S T A T E S

Seven Islands

Quebec

Montreal

Philadelphia

Hamilton

Cleveland

Detroit

Sault Ste. Marie

Port Arthur

Duluth

Milwaukee

Chicago

Principal steel areas
Important iron ore deposits
Shipping routes
Principal ports

0   300   Miles

98

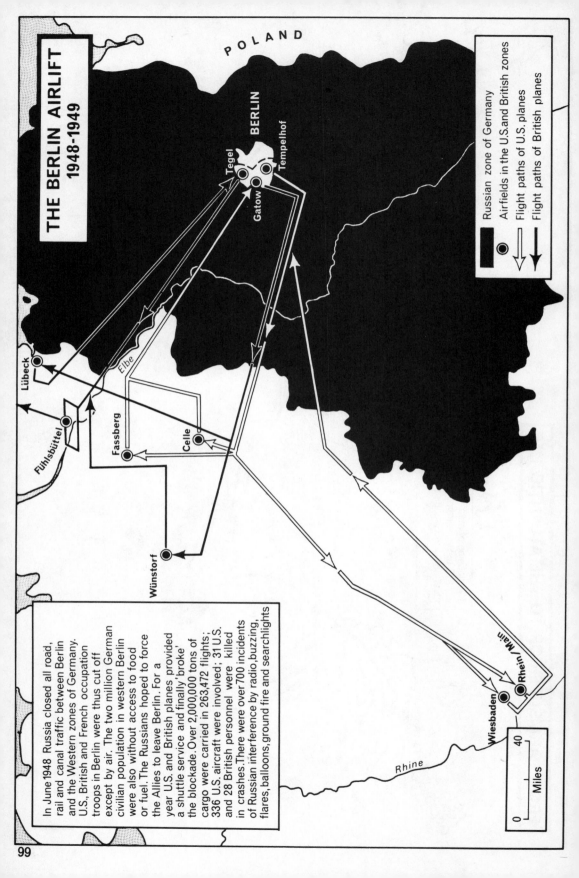

THE BERLIN AIRLIFT
1948-1949

P O L A N D

BERLIN

Tegel

Gatow

Tempelhof

Lübeck

Elbe

Fuhlsbüttel

Fassberg

Celle

Wünstorf

Rhein/Main

Wiesbaden

Rhine

Legend:
- Russian zone of Germany
- Airfields in the U.S. and British zones
- Flight paths of U.S. planes
- Flight paths of British planes

0   40
Miles

In June 1948 Russia closed all road, rail and canal traffic between Berlin and the Western zones of Germany. U.S., British and French occupation troops in Berlin were thus cut off except by air. The two million German civilian population in western Berlin were also without access to food or fuel. The Russians hoped to force the Allies to leave Berlin. For a year U.S. and British planes provided a shuttle service and finally 'broke' the blockade. Over 2,000,000 tons of cargo were carried in 263,472 flights; 336 U.S. aircraft were involved; 31 U.S. and 28 British personnel were killed in crashes. There were over 700 incidents of Russian interference by radio, buzzing, flares, balloons, ground fire and searchlights

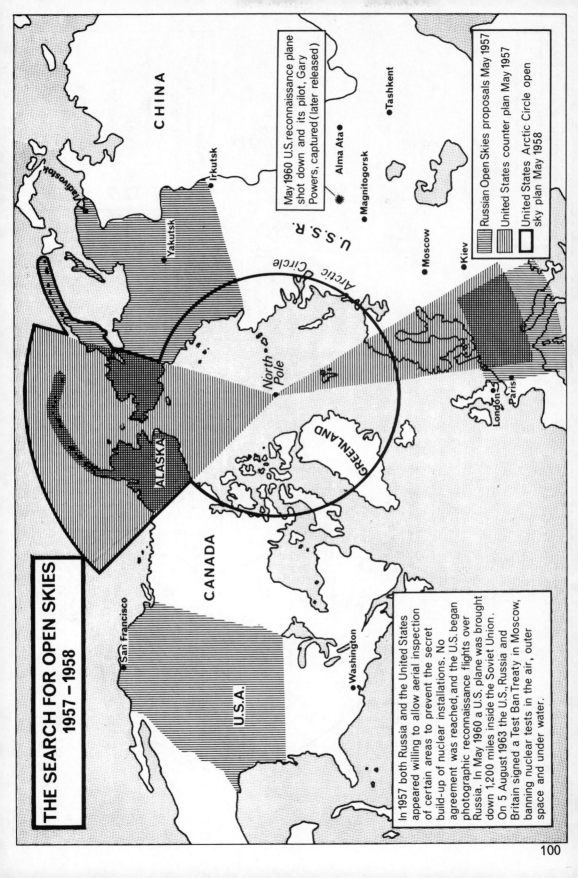

THE SEARCH FOR OPEN SKIES
1957 – 1958

C H I N A

U.S.S.R.

Vladivostok

Irkutsk

Yakutsk

Alma Ata

Magnitogorsk

Tashkent

Moscow

Kiev

May 1960 U.S. reconnaissance plane shot down and its pilot, Gary Powers, captured (later released)

Russian Open Skies proposals May 1957

United States counter plan May 1957

United States Arctic Circle open sky plan May 1958

Arctic Circle

North Pole

GREENLAND

London
Paris

ALASKA

CANADA

San Francisco

Washington

U.S.A.

In 1957 both Russia and the United States appeared willing to allow aerial inspection of certain areas to prevent the secret build-up of nuclear installations. No agreement was reached, and the U.S. began photographic reconnaissance flights over Russia. In May 1960 a U.S. plane was brought down 1,200 miles inside the Soviet Union. On 5 August 1963 the U.S., Russia and Britain signed a Test Ban Treaty in Moscow, banning nuclear tests in the air, outer space and under water.

100

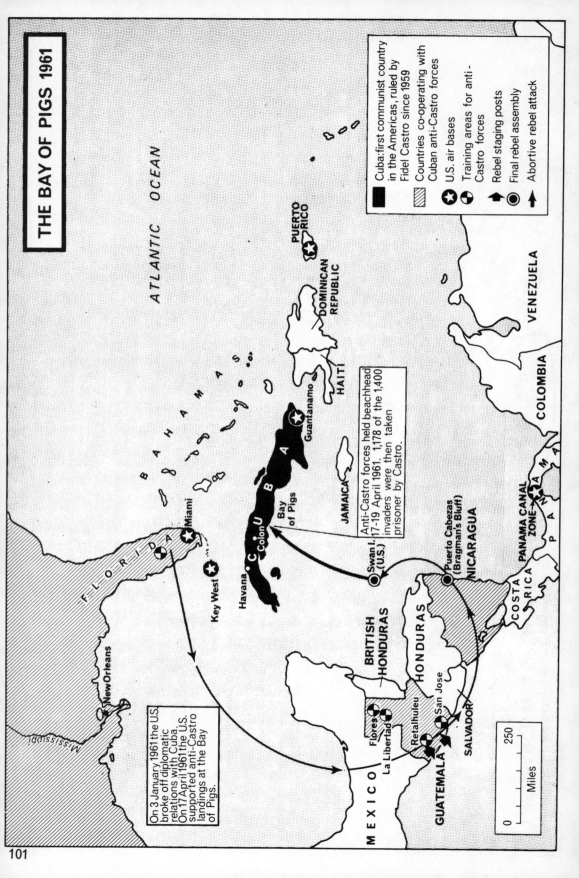

THE BAY OF PIGS 1961

ATLANTIC OCEAN

Cuba: first communist country in the Americas, ruled by Fidel Castro since 1959

Countries co-operating with Cuban anti-Castro forces

U.S. air bases

Training areas for anti-Castro forces

Rebel staging posts

Final rebel assembly

Abortive rebel attack

BAHAMAS

PUERTO RICO

DOMINICAN REPUBLIC

HAITI

C U B A

Guantanamo

Colon

Havana

Bay of Pigs

JAMAICA

Anti-Castro forces held beachhead 17-19 April 1961. 1,178 of the 1,400 invaders were then taken prisoner by Castro.

Swan I. (U.S.)

Miami

Key West

F L O R I D A

New Orleans

Mississippi

On 3 January 1961 the U.S. broke off diplomatic relations with Cuba. On 17 April 1961 the U.S. supported anti-Castro landings at the Bay of Pigs.

M E X I C O

Flores

La Libertad

GUATEMALA

Retalhuleu

San Jose

SALVADOR

BRITISH HONDURAS

HONDURAS

NICARAGUA

Puerto Cabezas (Bragman's Bluff)

COSTA RICA

PANAMA CANAL ZONE

PANAMA

COLOMBIA

VENEZUELA

0   250

Miles

101

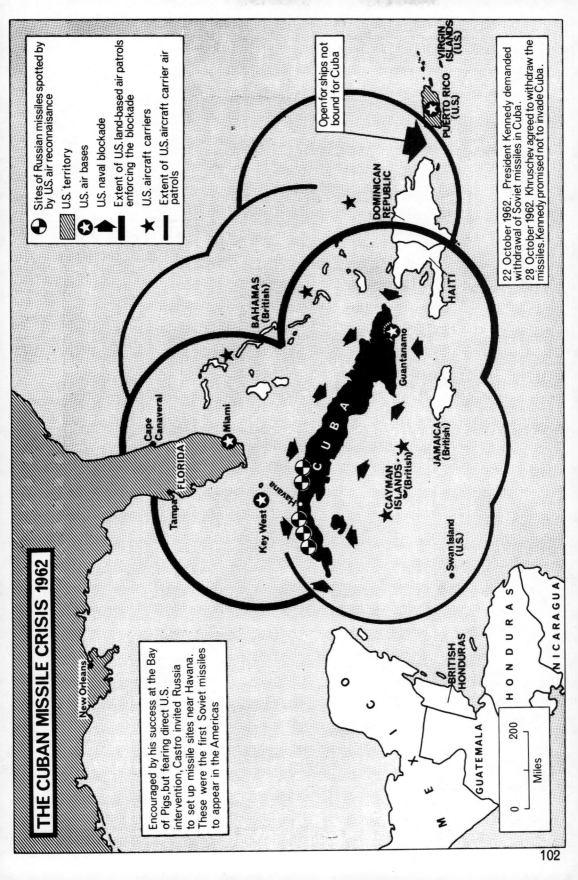

THE CUBAN MISSILE CRISIS 1962

Sites of Russian missiles spotted by U.S. air reconnaissance

U.S. territory

U.S. air bases

U.S. naval blockade

Extent of U.S. land-based air patrols enforcing the blockade

U.S. aircraft carriers

Extent of U.S. aircraft carrier air patrols

Open for ships not bound for Cuba.

22 October 1962. President Kennedy demanded withdrawal of Soviet missiles in Cuba.
28 October 1962. Khruschev agreed to withdraw the missiles. Kennedy promised not to invade Cuba.

Encouraged by his success at the Bay of Pigs, but fearing direct U.S. intervention, Castro invited Russia to set up missile sites near Havana. These were the first Soviet missiles to appear in the Americas.

New Orleans

FLORIDA

Cape Canaveral

Tampa

Miami

Key West

Havana

CUBA

BAHAMAS (British)

Guantanamo

JAMAICA (British)

CAYMAN ISLANDS (British)

Swan Island (U.S.)

HAITI

DOMINICAN REPUBLIC

PUERTO RICO (U.S.)

VIRGIN ISLANDS (U.S.)

MEXICO

GUATEMALA

BRITISH HONDURAS

HONDURAS

NICARAGUA

Miles

0   200

INDO-CHINA 1945-1954

Following the defeat of Japan in 1945, the Vietminh rebels opposed the return of French rule to Indo-China and demanded independence. The Vietminh, who were communist led, attacked the French. The U.S. paid France 78% of the cost of the war, 1953-1954. On 7 May 1954 French troops, besieged at Dien Bien Phu, surrendered. An armistice was signed on 21 July. "North" Vietnam went to the Vietminh and "South" Vietnam to a pro-French and pro-U.S. Government, following the Geneva Conference, April- July 1954.

CHINA

Red

Mekong

TONKIN

NORTH VIETNAM

Dien Bien Phu

Hanoi

Haiphong

BURMA

Mekong

Gulf
of
Tonkin

HAINAN
(China)

Luang
Prabang

Vientiane

LAOS

Vinh

ANNAM

Hué

Danang

SIAM

(THAILAND)

Quangngai

SOUTH VIETNAM

Binh Dinh

Bangkok

Mekong

CAMBODIA

Dalat

Pnompenh

Phanrang

COCHIN CHINA

Saigon

Boundary of French Indo-China
Controlled by Vietminh : 1946-1950
Gained by Vietminh : 1952-1954
◆◆◆◆ Vietnam as divided into North and South by the Geneva Conference of 1954

0   150
Miles

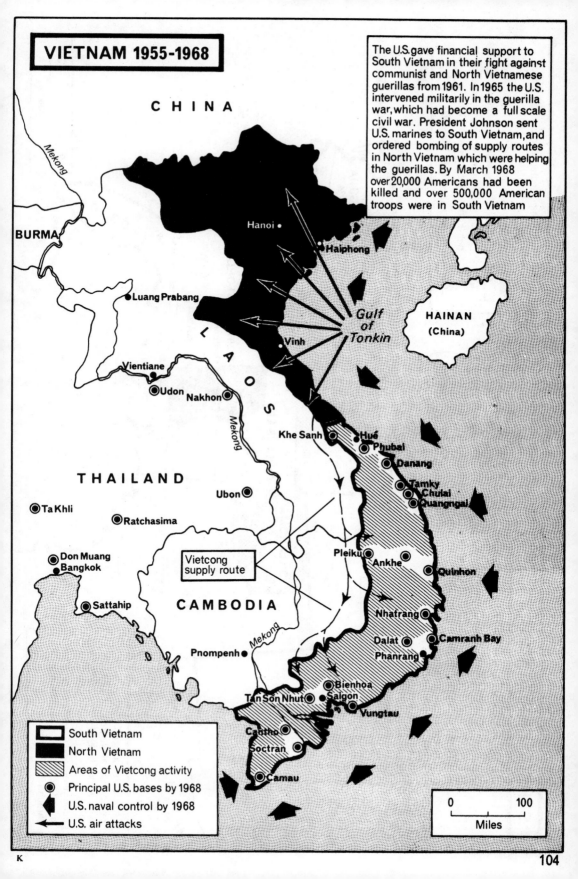

VIETNAM 1955-1968

CHINA

The U.S. gave financial support to South Vietnam in their fight against communist and North Vietnamese guerillas from 1961. In 1965 the U.S. intervened militarily in the guerilla war, which had become a full scale civil war. President Johnson sent U.S. marines to South Vietnam, and ordered bombing of supply routes in North Vietnam which were helping the guerillas. By March 1968 over 20,000 Americans had been killed and over 500,000 American troops were in South Vietnam

BURMA

Mekong

Hanoi

Haiphong

Luang Prabang

LAOS

Vinh

Gulf of Tonkin

HAINAN (China)

Vientiane

Udon

Nakhon

Mekong

THAILAND

Ubon

Khe Sanh

Hué
Phubai
Danang
Tamky
Chulai
Quangngai

Ta Khli

Ratchasima

Pleiku

Ankhe

Quinhon

Don Muang
Bangkok

CAMBODIA

Vietcong supply route

Nhatrang

Sattahip

Mekong

Dalat

Phanrang

Camranh Bay

Pnompenh

Bienhoa
Tan Son Nhut
Saigon
Vungtau

Cantho

Soctran

Camau

South Vietnam

North Vietnam

Areas of Vietcong activity

Principal U.S. bases by 1968

U.S. naval control by 1968

U.S. air attacks

0   100

Miles

K

104

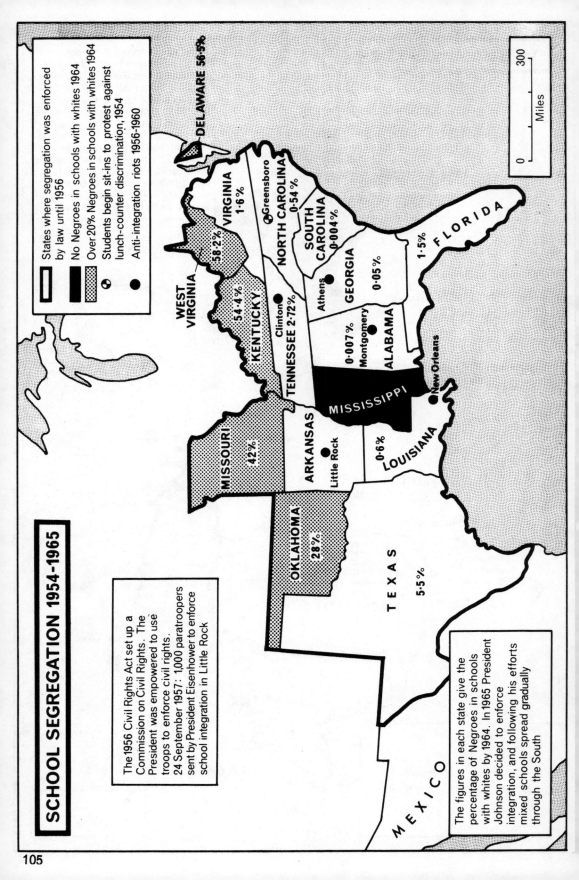

SCHOOL SEGREGATION 1954–1965

Legend:
- States where segregation was enforced by law until 1956
- No Negroes in schools with whites 1964
- Over 20% Negroes in schools with whites 1964
- Students begin sit-ins to protest against lunch-counter discrimination, 1954
- Anti-integration riots 1956–1960

Scale: 0 — 300 Miles

State figures (percentage of Negroes in schools with whites by 1964):

- DELAWARE 56·5%
- VIRGINIA 1·6%
- WEST VIRGINIA 58·2%
- NORTH CAROLINA 0·54%
- SOUTH CAROLINA 0·004%
- GEORGIA 0·05%
- FLORIDA 1·5%
- KENTUCKY 54·4%
- TENNESSEE 2·72%
- ALABAMA 0·007%
- MISSISSIPPI
- MISSOURI 42%
- ARKANSAS
- LOUISIANA 0·6%
- OKLAHOMA 28%
- TEXAS 5·5%

Cities/places marked: Greensboro, Athens, Clinton, Montgomery, New Orleans, Little Rock

MEXICO

The 1956 Civil Rights Act set up a Commission on Civil Rights. The President was empowered to use troops to enforce civil rights.
24 September 1957: 1,000 paratroopers sent by President Eisenhower to enforce school integration in Little Rock

The figures in each state give the percentage of Negroes in schools with whites by 1964. In 1965 President Johnson decided to enforce integration, and following his efforts mixed schools spread gradually through the South

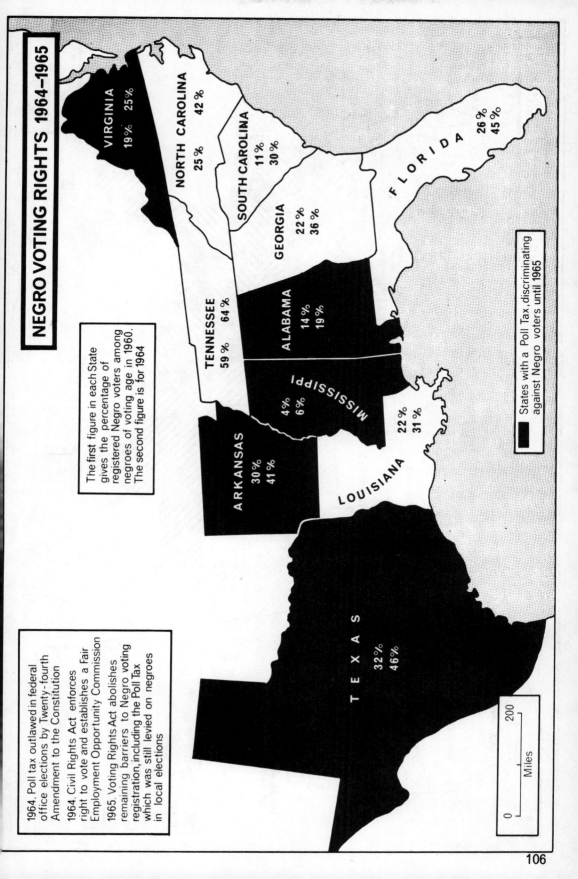

NEGRO VOTING RIGHTS 1964–1965

VIRGINIA
19% 25%

NORTH CAROLINA
25% 42%

SOUTH CAROLINA
11% 30%

GEORGIA
22% 36%

FLORIDA
26% 45%

TENNESSEE
59% 64%

ALABAMA
14% 19%

MISSISSIPPI
4% 6%

ARKANSAS
30% 41%

LOUISIANA
22% 31%

TEXAS
32% 46%

The first figure in each State gives the percentage of registered Negro voters among negroes of voting age in 1960. The second figure is for 1964

1964. Poll tax outlawed in federal office elections by Twenty-fourth Amendment to the Constitution

1964. Civil Rights Act enforces right to vote and establishes a Fair Employment Opportunity Commission

1965. Voting Rights Act abolishes remaining barriers to Negro voting registration, including the Poll Tax which was still levied on negroes in local elections

■ States with a Poll Tax, discriminating against Negro voters until 1965

0 200

Miles

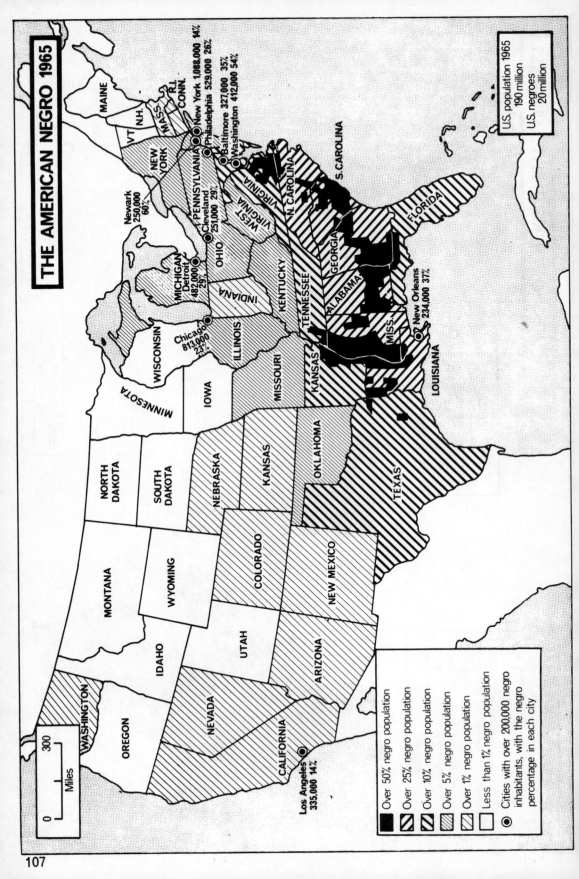

THE AMERICAN NEGRO 1965

U.S. population 1965
190 million
U.S. negroes
20 million

New York 1,088,000 14%
Philadelphia 529,000 26%
Baltimore 327,000 35%
Washington 412,000 54%
Newark 250,000 60%
Cleveland 251,000 29%
Detroit 482,000 29%
Chicago 813,000 23%
New Orleans 234,000 37%
Los Angeles 335,000 14%

Over 50% negro population
Over 25% negro population
Over 10% negro population
Over 5% negro population
Over 1% negro population
Less than 1% negro population
Cities with over 200,000 negro inhabitants, with the negro percentage in each city

Miles
0   300

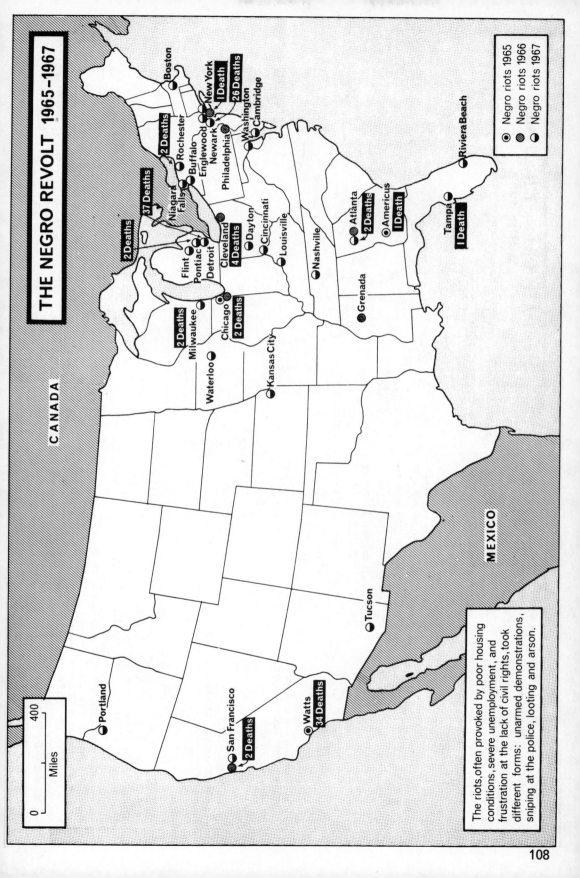

THE NEGRO REVOLT 1965-1967

CANADA

MEXICO

Miles
0   400

Negro riots 1965
Negro riots 1966
Negro riots 1967

Boston
New York   1 Death
26 Deaths
Washington
Cambridge
Riviera Beach
2 Deaths Rochester
Buffalo
Englewood Newark
Philadelphia
37 Deaths Niagara Falls
Atlanta   2 Deaths
Americus 1 Death
Cleveland Dayton
Cincinnati   Tampa 1 Death
2 Deaths   Flint   4 Deaths Louisville
Pontiac Detroit
Nashville
Milwaukee   Grenada
2 Deaths   Chicago   2 Deaths
Waterloo
Kansas City

Tucson

Portland
San Francisco
2 Deaths
Watts
34 Deaths

The riots, often provoked by poor housing conditions, severe unemployment, and frustration at the lack of civil rights, took different forms: unarmed demonstrations, sniping at the police, looting and arson.

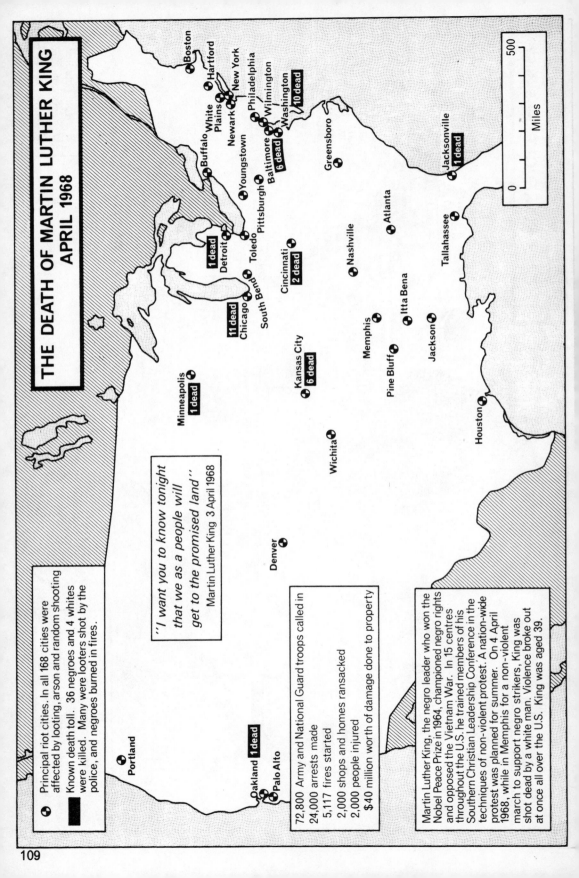

THE DEATH OF MARTIN LUTHER KING
APRIL 1968

"I want you to know tonight that we as a people will get to the promised land"
Martin Luther King 3 April 1968

- Principal riot cities. In all 168 cities were affected by looting, arson and random shooting
- Known death toll. 36 negroes and 4 whites were killed. Many were looters shot by the police, and negroes burned in fires.

72,800 Army and National Guard troops called in
24,000 arrests made
5,117 fires started
2,000 shops and homes ransacked
2,000 people injured
$40 million worth of damage done to property

Martin Luther King, the negro leader who won the Nobel Peace Prize in 1964, championed negro rights and opposed the U.S. Vietnam War. In 15 centres throughout the U.S. he trained members of his Southern Christian Leadership Conference in the techniques of non-violent protest. A nation-wide protest was planned for summer. On 4 April 1968, while in Memphis for a non-violent march to support negro strikers, King was shot dead by a white man. Violence broke out at once all over the U.S. King was aged 39.

Boston
Hartford
New York
Buffalo
White Plains
Newark
Philadelphia
Wilmington
Washington **10 dead**
Youngstown
Baltimore **6 dead**
Pittsburgh
Greensboro
Jacksonville **1 dead**
Detroit **1 dead**
Toledo
Atlanta
South Bend
Chicago **11 dead**
Cincinnati **2 dead**
Nashville
Tallahassee
Itta Bena
Memphis
Jackson
Kansas City **6 dead**
Pine Bluff
Minneapolis **1 dead**
Wichita
Houston
Denver
Portland
Oakland **1 dead**
Palo Alto

500
Miles
0

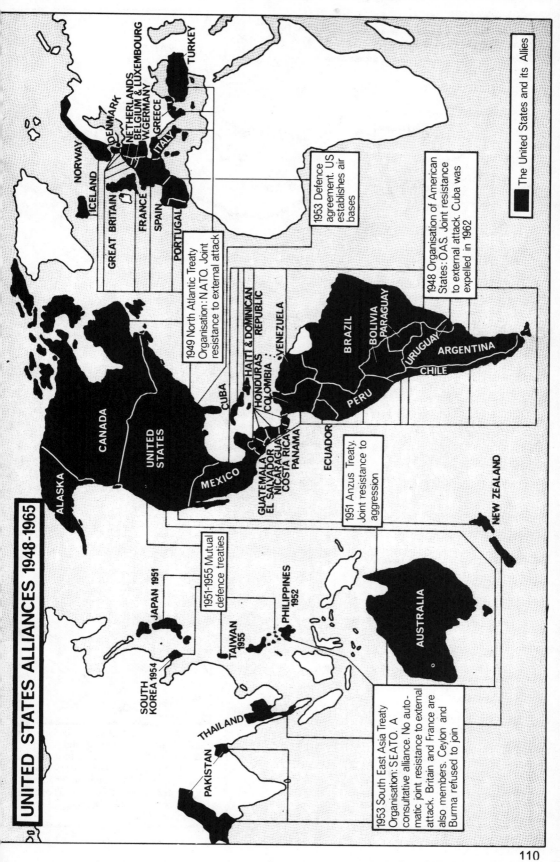

UNITED STATES ALLIANCES 1948-1965

The United States and its Allies

NORWAY
ICELAND
DENMARK
NETHERLANDS
BELGIUM & LUXEMBOURG
W.GERMANY
GREECE
ITALY
TURKEY

GREAT BRITAIN
FRANCE
SPAIN
PORTUGAL

1949 North Atlantic Treaty Organisation: N.A.T.O. Joint resistance to external attack

1953 Defence agreement. US establishes air bases

1948 Organisation of American States: OAS. Joint resistance to external attack. Cuba was expelled in 1962

ALASKA

CANADA

UNITED STATES

MEXICO

GUATEMALA
EL SALVADOR
COSTA RICA
PANAMA

CUBA

HAITI & DOMINICAN REPUBLIC
HONDURAS
COLOMBIA
NICARAGUA
VENEZUELA

ECUADOR

PERU

BRAZIL
BOLIVIA
PARAGUAY
CHILE
URUGUAY
ARGENTINA

JAPAN 1951

SOUTH KOREA 1954

TAIWAN 1955

PHILIPPINES 1952

1951-1955 Mutual defence treaties

1951 Anzus Treaty. Joint resistance to aggression

NEW ZEALAND

AUSTRALIA

PAKISTAN

THAILAND

1953 South East Asia Treaty Organisation: SEATO. A consultative alliance. No auto-matic joint resistance to external attack. Britain and France are also members. Ceylon and Burma refused to join

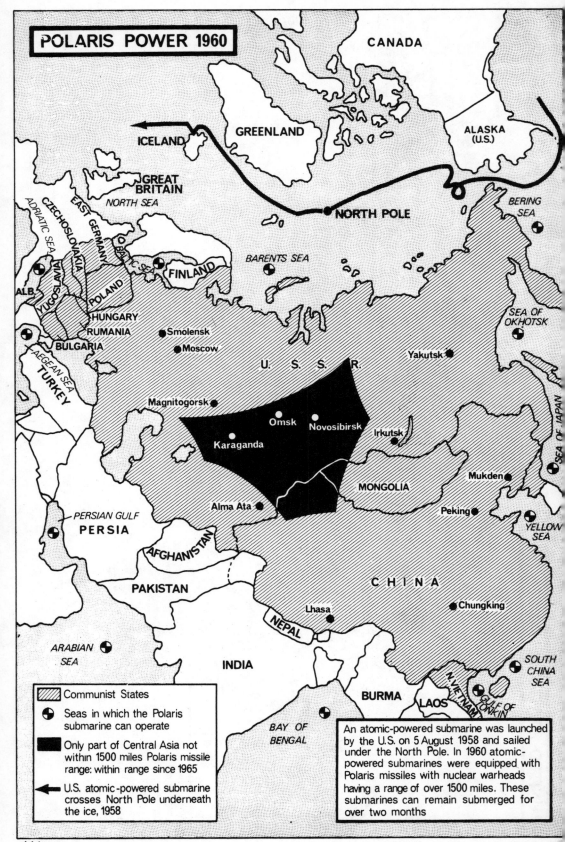

POLARIS POWER 1960

CANADA

GREENLAND

ICELAND

ALASKA (U.S.)

GREAT BRITAIN

NORTH SEA

BERING SEA

NORTH POLE

BARENTS SEA

ADRIATIC SEA

CZECHOSLOVAKIA

EAST GERMANY

BALTIC SEA

FINLAND

ALB.

POLAND

YUGOSLAVIA

HUNGARY

RUMANIA

BULGARIA

Smolensk

Moscow

U. S. S. R.

Yakutsk

SEA OF OKHOTSK

AEGEAN SEA

TURKEY

Magnitogorsk

Omsk

Novosibirsk

Irkutsk

SEA OF JAPAN

Karaganda

MONGOLIA

Mukden

PERSIAN GULF

PERSIA

Alma Ata

Peking

YELLOW SEA

AFGHANISTAN

PAKISTAN

C H I N A

Chungking

Lhasa

NEPAL

ARABIAN SEA

INDIA

BURMA

LAOS

SOUTH CHINA SEA

N.VIETNAM

GULF OF TONKIN

BAY OF BENGAL

Communist States

Seas in which the Polaris submarine can operate

Only part of Central Asia not within 1500 miles Polaris missile range: within range since 1965

U.S. atomic-powered submarine crosses North Pole underneath the ice, 1958

An atomic-powered submarine was launched by the U.S. on 5 August 1958 and sailed under the North Pole. In 1960 atomic-powered submarines were equipped with Polaris missiles with nuclear warheads having a range of over 1500 miles. These submarines can remain submerged for over two months

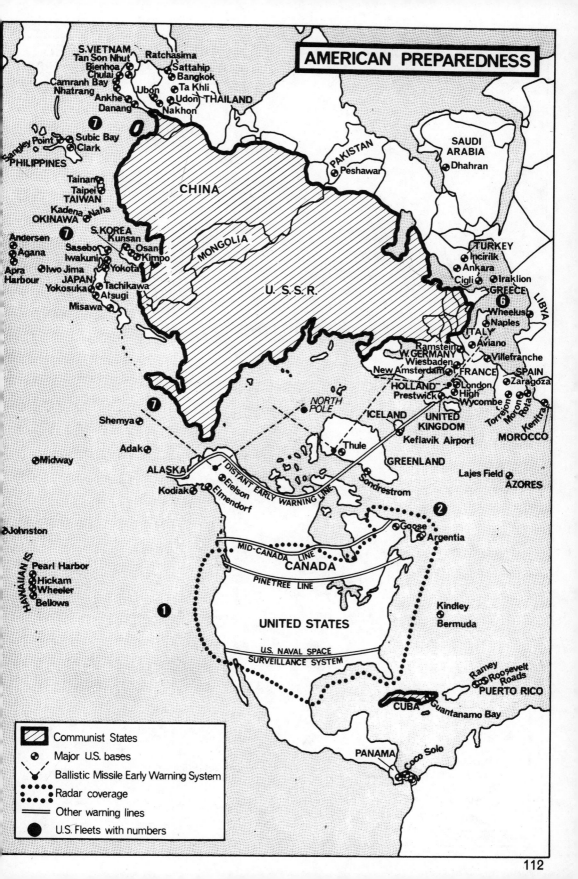

AMERICAN PREPAREDNESS

S.VIETNAM
Tan Son Nhut
Bienhoa
Camranh Bay
Nhatrang
Ankhe
Danang
Ratchasima
Sattahip
Bangkok
Ta Khli
Ubon
Udon **THAILAND**
Nakhon
Chulai

PAKISTAN
Peshawar

SAUDI ARABIA
Dhahran

CHINA

MONGOLIA

U. S. S. R.

❼

⓿

Sangley Point
Subic Bay
Clark
PHILIPPINES

Tainan
Taipei
TAIWAN
Kadena
Naha
OKINAWA
Andersen
Agana
Apra
Harbour
S.KOREA Kunsan
Sasebo Osan
Iwakuni Kimpo
Iwo Jima Yokota
JAPAN
Yokosuka Tachikawa
Atsugi
Misawa

❼

TURKEY
Incirlik
Ankara
Cigli
Iraklion
GREECE
Wheelus
Naples
LIBYA
Aviano
ITALY
Ramstein Villefranche
W.GERMANY
Wiesbaden
New Amsterdam **FRANCE**
HOLLAND London **SPAIN**
Prestwick High Zaragoza
Wycombe
Torrejon Moron Rota
MOROCCO Kenitra

❻

Shemya

❼

NORTH POLE

ICELAND
Keflavik Airport
UNITED KINGDOM

Adak

Thule

GREENLAND

Midway

ALASKA
Kodiak
Eielson
Elmendorf

DISTANT EARLY WARNING LINE

Sondrestrom

Lajes Field
AZORES

Johnston

Goose
Argentia

❷

Pearl Harbor
Hickam
Wheeler
Bellows
HAWAIIAN IS.

MID-CANADA LINE

CANADA

PINETREE LINE

❶

Kindley
Bermuda

UNITED STATES

U.S. NAVAL SPACE SURVEILLANCE SYSTEM

Ramey
Roosevelt Roads
PUERTO RICO

CUBA Guantanamo Bay

PANAMA
Coco Solo

▨	Communist States
☉	Major U.S. bases
⟋⟍	Ballistic Missile Early Warning System
•••••	Radar coverage
═══	Other warning lines
●	U.S. Fleets with numbers

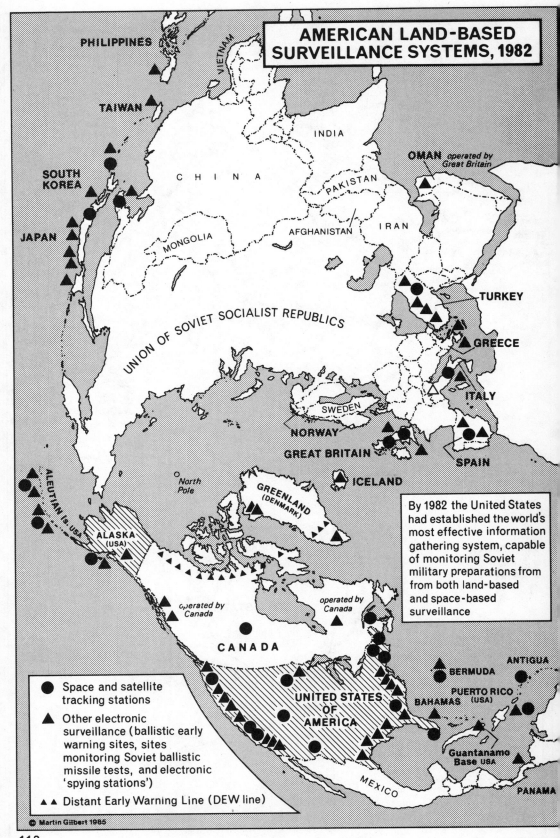

AMERICAN LAND-BASED SURVEILLANCE SYSTEMS, 1982

PHILIPPINES

VIETNAM

TAIWAN

INDIA

OMAN *operated by Great Britain*

SOUTH KOREA

C H I N A

PAKISTAN

JAPAN

MONGOLIA

AFGHANISTAN

IRAN

TURKEY

GREECE

UNION OF SOVIET SOCIALIST REPUBLICS

ITALY

SWEDEN

NORWAY

GREAT BRITAIN

ICELAND

SPAIN

ALEUTIAN Is. USA

North Pole

GREENLAND (DENMARK)

By 1982 the United States had established the world's most effective information gathering system, capable of monitoring Soviet military preparations from from both land-based and space-based surveillance

ALASKA (USA)

operated by Canada

operated by Canada

ANTIGUA

C A N A D A

BERMUDA

PUERTO RICO (USA)

UNITED STATES OF AMERICA

BAHAMAS

● Space and satellite tracking stations

▲ Other electronic surveillance (ballistic early warning sites, sites monitoring Soviet ballistic missile tests, and electronic 'spying stations')

Guantanamo Base USA

MEXICO

PANAMA

▲▲ Distant Early Warning Line (DEW line)

© Martin Gilbert 1985

THE UNITED STATES AND THE SOVIET UNION IN OUTER SPACE

Between 1957 and 1981 a total of 2,725 satellites were launched, most of them by the United States and the Soviet Union. Some of the principal satellites in orbit in 1981 are shown here. In March 1981 the US National Aeronautics and Space Administration (NASA) launched its Columbia Orbiter, the first re-usable space vehicle (44 missions planned by the end of 1985, nine of them military)

SATELLITES

Early Warning
USA   22
USSR 25

Communications
USA   118
USSR 366
NATO   5
UK   4
France 2

Photographic reconnaisance
USA   235
USSR   538
China   3

Electronic reconnaisance
USA   790
USSR   125

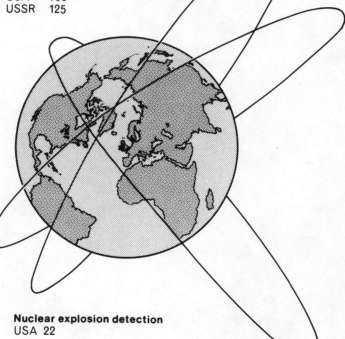

Navigation
USA   39
USSR 25

Ocean surveillance
USA   18
USSR 32

Nuclear explosion detection
USA 22

Interception - destruction
USSR 33

In January 1985, at Geneva, the United States and the Soviet Union agreed to begin talks aimed at an agreement over the restriction of warfare in outer space. The United States was involved in the development of anti-satellite missiles and anti-missile lasers, and the Soviet Union in anti-satellite satellites

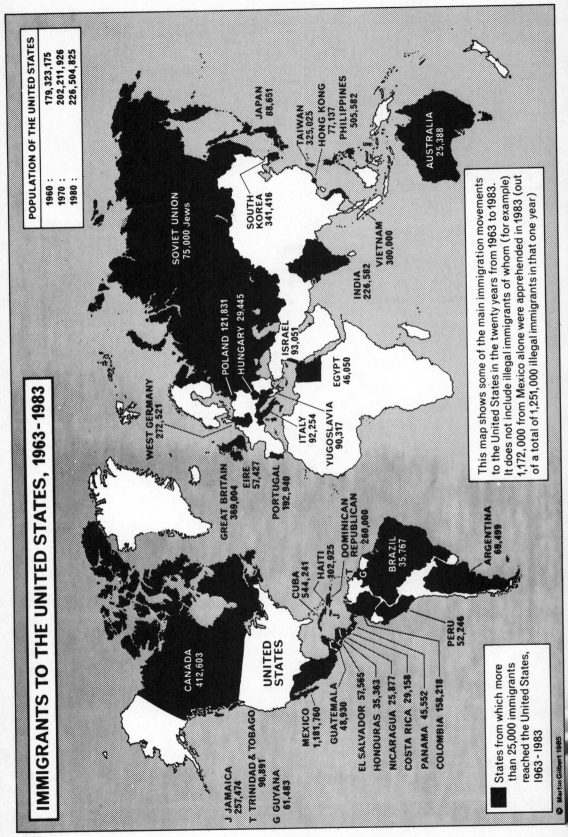

IMMIGRANTS TO THE UNITED STATES, 1963 - 1983

POPULATION OF THE UNITED STATES	
1960 :	179,323,175
1970 :	202,211,926
1980 :	226,504,825

SOVIET UNION
75,000 Jews

JAPAN
88,651

TAIWAN
325,025

HONG KONG
77,137

PHILIPPINES
505,582

AUSTRALIA
25,388

SOUTH KOREA
341,416

VIETNAM
300,000

INDIA
226,582

POLAND 121,831

HUNGARY 29,445

ISRAEL
93,051

EGYPT
46,050

WEST GERMANY
272,521

ITALY
92,254

YUGOSLAVIA
90,317

GREAT BRITAIN
369,004

EIRE
57,427

PORTUGAL
102,940

CANADA
412,603

UNITED STATES

J JAMAICA
257,474

T TRINIDAD & TOBAGO
90,891

G GUYANA
61,483

MEXICO
1,181,760

GUATEMALA
48,930

EL SALVADOR 57,565

HONDURAS 35,363

NICARAGUA 25,877

COSTA RICA 29,158

PANAMA 45,552

COLOMBIA 158,218

CUBA
544,241

HAITI
102,925

DOMINICAN REPUBLIC
260,000

BRAZIL
35,767

PERU
52,746

ARGENTINA
68,499

This map shows some of the main immigration movements to the United States in the twenty years from 1963 to 1983. It does not include illegal immigrants of whom (for example) 1,172,000 from Mexico alone were apprehended in 1983 (out of a total of 1,251,000 illegal immigrants in that one year)

■ States from which more than 25,000 immigrants reached the United States, 1963 - 1983

© Martin Gilbert 1985

115